FOOTBALL:
Six of the Best

FOOTBALL:
Six of the Best

Alan Hansen
with Trevor Haylett

Hodder & Stoughton

First published in Great Britain in 1996
by Hodder and Stoughton
A division of Hodder Headline PLC

British Library Cataloguing in Publication Data
Hansen, Alan
Football: six of the best
1. Soccer players 2. Soccer
I. Title
796.3'34'0922

ISBN 0 340 66629 3

Typeset by Palimpsest Book Production Limited,
Polmont, Stirlingshire
Printed and bound in Great Britain by
Mackays of Chatham PLC, Chatham, Kent

Hodder and Stoughton
A division of Hodder Headline PLC
338 Euston Road
London NW1 3BH

CONTENTS

ACKNOWLEDGEMENTS

I would like to thank Trevor Haylett, who for the past ten years has written on football for the *Daily Mail*, the *Independent* and other publications, for his help in putting this book together. He was there to jog the memory and to make a case for those players I had omitted.

INTRODUCTION

It's a game we have all played at some time or other, with our mates either at school or maybe around the bar, or on our own to while away an empty hour or two. Someone says: 'Who was the best striker/goalkeeper/playmaker you have ever seen, what have been the most exciting matches?' and so the debate begins and the arguments start. We all agree football is a game of opinions yet not often do those opinions agree.

Over the next 184 pages I have selected those who, in my opinion, over the last twenty-five years have been the outstanding players in their positions. In each category I have divided British and Irish players into two eras, from 1990–95 and from 1970–89, and chosen my top six. Then I name the best from those twelve names and a Rest of the World top six from 1970–95. Finally, I select the *crème de la crème* – I call them my Super Six – the best from home and abroad over the entire twenty-five-year period. How many do you agree with?

The tables are set out at the end of each chapter. Preceding them, I have considered each player in turn and explained just why they make the grade. The order in which they appear is not necessarily their rating in the table so you are left guessing until the end of the chapter as to who comes out ahead.

I have also looked at other areas of the game and listed what I believe to be the greatest games of the last twenty-five years, the greatest goals, the finest achievements, the young players likely to make the most impact, the best signings from abroad etc. etc. Mostly I have rated them from 1 to 6, in some chapters they are listed in no particular order of importance.

Make your own selections as you go through the book and see how your opinions compare with mine. I had fun; I'm sure you will too.

For those of you who are not Liverpool supporters, it may seem that there is a surfeit of candidates from my old club. Forgive me, but these are the players I know best. And, for a large part of the last twenty-five years, Liverpool was the foremost club side in England.

SUPER STRIKERS

There are great goalscorers and then there are great strikers who are not necessarily prolific at finding the net. I would much rather be facing the out-and-out marksman than the guy with the superior game who I knew would give me problems from start to finish without necessarily finishing up on the scoresheet.

The prodigious finisher is a deceptive player. I have walked off the pitch having faced a Gary Lineker or a Clive Allen, satisfied that they had not done much in the game and I had kept them quiet. Then you'd glance up at the list of scorers and there they would be, their name in lights again. It may have been a goalmouth scramble and at the time you would be uncertain who had secured the final touch but like all penalty box kings, they were there when it mattered.

Mark Hughes stands out among those who guarantee you a torrid afternoon irrespective of whether he troubles the scorers. Someone once memorably said that Hughes was a scorer of great goals but not a great goalscorer and that sums him up.

Neither Hughes nor Graeme Sharp were 30-goals-a-season men but they led the line so well you couldn't relax for a moment. When the ball was played up to them they were skilled at holding it up, waiting for support to arrive.

Goalscoring is a highly prized gift and anyone who scores 49 in a season as Clive Allen did in the 1986–87 season is a tremendous asset. The down side is that they might not be able to offer you anything else. If your side is under pressure and the goalscorer is unable to do anything to help, unable to retain possession and give the defensive players a breather, then you're really functioning with a man short.

The big difference between the British striker and those who play abroad is the quality of the movement. The worst – or best – I ever faced in that respect was the German, Karl-Heinz Rummenigge. Liverpool played Bayern Munich in the semi-final of the 1980–81 European Cup and Rummenigge was absolutely brilliant at running across you the moment the ball was played. It was very disconcerting and it was a good job I was quick because over the two games I just couldn't get used to it. Others would run before or after the ball was kicked and occasionally they might get it spot on. Incredibly, Rummenigge was right every single time.

I've considered 1970–89 under the heading of strikers, 1990–95 under the heading of goalscorers. Drawing this distinction means that Gary Lineker is excluded from the earlier group because he was an out-and-out goalscorer while others like Hughes and Kenny Dalglish, for instance, offered more to the team. Ian Rush is a combination of the two, he scores an incredible number of goals but also leads the line well; he makes both lists.

In both instances I've had to leave out a number of good players, big target men like Joe Jordan and Joe Royle, Allan Clarke at Leeds, the Arsenal pair of John Radford and Ray Kennedy, Frank Stapleton who gave great service to both Arsenal and Manchester United. From the modern era, Les Ferdinand came close but before the 1995–96 season he had not been a prolific scorer, while Ally McCoist deserves recognition, even though he, too, did not make it.

British and Irish goalscorers
1990–95

Alan Shearer

Shearer reminds me of Dalglish with his amazing strength and his ability to push people out of the way. He has been the best in this country for the last few years; tremendously hard-working and full of determination allied to a sharp instinct for knowing just where the goal is.

Shearer's a great team player but when it comes to scoring goals he is very single-minded. In his position he has to be. Anything within distance and you can see him thinking 'I'm hitting this'.

What I like about him – and this was another Dalglish characteristic – is that when things are not going well he is working even harder for his team. That appetite and enthusiasm is what separates the truly great players from those who are merely very good.

Shearer's impact on Blackburn, the club and the team, cannot be overstated. He had a catalytic effect on the whole revolution there because without him showing his faith in Dalglish's ability to transform the club, other ambitious players would not have agreed to join.

Ian Rush

It's not only the number of goals Rush scores, it's the way he leads the line, his phenomenal work-rate. He is the first line of defence through the pressure he exerts on his opponents. In fact he started the concept of defending from the front. With Dalglish putting his foot in and Rush terrorising alongside, the partnership was awesome. One particular season, I had a bad six months and I'm convinced he was the cause. In training games, if the ball was played into the defence you'd not be looking at it, you'd be worrying about Rush. It damaged my confidence.

In 1985 I was on the bench for a Scotland v Wales World Cup

qualifying tie when Mark Hughes and Rush produced the best display of forward play I have ever seen. It frightened the life out of me just sitting on the touchline. You had Hughes with his bullish aggression and Rush with his speed and his ability to work all night. He also scored a wonderful goal from 25 yards.

John Aldridge

If you were going to stake your life on one player always being in the box on the end of a cross, that man would be Aldridge. He was quite exceptional for that – right wing, left wing, high ball, low ball, he would be in there hungrily hunting it down, and it remains the case at Tranmere where he has continued his remarkable goalscoring feats.

Yet I can also say that John was one of the worst five-a-side players I've ever come across. If you saw him in training games at Melwood you would think, this is not a footballer. If I didn't go past him six times I would be disappointed. Put him out on a Saturday, however, and he would always get you goals, great goals at that for he was a talented striker and dominant in the air as well. He had incredible strength and the courage to get in where it hurts which endures to this day.

When strikers pass 30, more often than not it's their courage that is the first to go. You've spent ten years with your back to defenders, being kicked from pillar to post and after a time enough is enough. The inclination is not to be brave any more. Aldo is the exception to the rule.

Ian Wright

Wright is blessed with extraordinary pace and when I first played against him I thought that's all he had. But in recent seasons I have seen him accumulate some outstanding goals which could only be the product of a player with supreme talent. Wright can find the net any way he chooses – he can hit it with either foot, with power or, more subtly, with accuracy; he can also pack away a good volley.

The goal he scored for Arsenal against Southampton early in the 1995–96 season, when he twisted his defender into all kinds of knots before steering the ball delicately past the goalkeeper, encapsulated everything about him: great talent plus an awareness of where other players are – not only his team-mates but the keeper as well.

Ian has failed to make an impact for England and because of that it is said he falls just short of the highest standards. I'm not so sure that's fair. Strikers are always judged on the goals they score and you can be unlucky to come into a side at a time when it is going through a bad patch and the service to the front players is poor. In international football, the nature of the beast is such that after a poor run the cry goes up for heads to roll. It seems to me that Ian has missed out through no fault of his own.

Gary Lineker

Lineker's scoring rate was phenomenal, not only in English football but also for the England team.

When he first emerged, with his reputation built on the ball over the top and his electrifying pace, you would never have guessed Gary would become a prolific scorer for his country, because it is much more difficult in international football where most teams operate with a sweeper. That he maintained and added to his goalscoring rate showed how much he learned as he matured. He got better and better at finding space and exploiting it.

Around the mid-eighties when Liverpool and Everton were involved in stirring encounters, there was no one quicker. I was fast but I couldn't catch him. You don't mind facing a player with pace if that's all he has. You don't mind someone with height if there's nothing else in his armoury. Lineker had pace, great finishing skills and the ability to be in the right place at the right time, and his markers always had their hands full.

Every facet of Lineker's game was positive. If you were a defender bringing the ball under control he would be moving behind anticipating the mistake. Nine times out of ten the defender would be OK but Lineker found a lot of goals that way.

This is a very competitive group of goalscorers, but Gary gets in at number one because of his vast tally of goals for England. That puts him ahead of both Rush, who has suffered because Wales have never made an impact on the world stage, and Shearer who so far has not shown that he can be an outstanding scorer at the very highest level.

Andy Cole

Not yet the finished article, Cole warrants a place in this line-up because his record for Newcastle was exceptional. Another player where it's a case of stick the ball in front of him and invariably it ends up in the net. His pace is devastating.

When Cole shoots it's always hard and true. Ninety-nine per cent of his goals are scored that way and I think he's got to learn a trick from Peter Beardsley and vary it.

At the end of the 1994–95 season, Manchester United had to beat West Ham to win the championship. With a minute to go, Cole only had to get the ball past Ludek Miklosko for the title to stay at Old Trafford.

He hit it hard and low and the goalkeeper, who seemed to have been down anticipating the shot for a good three minutes, made the save. A little dink and Miklosko couldn't have got to it. But Andy's still only 24 and it's easy to be over-critical. He is improving all the time with his back to goal and time is on his side.

British and Irish strikers
1970–89

Mark Hughes

The way I tend to judge a player is to ask myself if I would have liked to play alongside him at Liverpool. Hughes passes the test every time.

It has been strange to see him doing all those things we expect from him – holding the ball up, shaking defenders off, scoring his spectacular volleys – in Chelsea blue rather than Manchester United red.

It's become harder for strikers because it seems they are only judged now on the number of goals they score and in that regard Hughes loses marks. He is never going to be a 30-goals-a-season man.

He does not pick up enough of the bread-and-butter goals, the tap-ins from close in, but despite that he is still one of the best of his era.

Kenny Dalglish

A great goalscorer, Dalglish was also a first-class provider of goals and took delight in setting them up for other people.

Because he didn't have any pace to start with, Kenny could have played on for ever. Bob Paisley used to say that at the top level the first two yards were in your head and the longer I was involved in the game the more I came to realise he was absolutely right. Kenny was quicker over the first two yards than anyone else in the country. He read the game so well you could pass the ball three yards either side of him and still be completely confident he would be first on to it, no matter how tightly he was marked.

Sharp in everything he did, Dalglish was inventive, creative, and as strong as an ox. Kick him up the backside and he would come back for more.

He had a massive desire to win, individually and collectively. You would see it in five-a-sides, tiddlywinks, anything. He might be having a bad time – and there weren't many of those – yet there he was in the 89th minute trying even harder than he was in the first.

Graeme Sharp

Sharp formed a devastating partnership with Andy Gray and was essential to Everton's success in the eighties. Highly underrated, he was the focal point of every Everton attack. He was not a prolific goalscorer but that was because he was totally unselfish. If there was a player in a better position, Sharpie would always pick him out. How many times did we see him at the back-post knocking balls across for someone else in a blue shirt to force home, and he forfeited a lot of personal glory that way.

As a centre-forward backing into defenders to earn free-kicks, he was without peer. When Liverpool played Everton it always ended up a screaming match: our bench would be shouting for the foul as Sharp backed in on me, their bench would be claiming the decision because I was blocking him.

It was a clever ploy on his part because eventually, no matter how many free-kicks went against him, Everton would get a decision around the penalty area; with the ability of someone like Kevin Sheedy to bend the ball around the defensive wall, it often led to goals.

Kevin Keegan

Keegan is always portrayed as the striker who made the most of a limited amount of ability. He worked his socks off, it's true, but that won't lead to much unless you have ability to go with it. It is impossible to achieve what he did in the game without craft and know-how.

Kevin had the lot: strength, power, good ability in the air for his height, a superb all-round game combined with an incredible hunger and energy for hard labour. Physically and mentally he was equipped to compete at any level.

I only faced him three or four times when he came back from Germany and signed for Southampton and then later switched to Newcastle. What struck me immediately was his movement, his intelligent runs. After five minutes I was thinking 'thank your lucky stars you weren't around when this man was at his peak.' He was not as quick then but his movement was deadly. It is something you are born with, the intelligence to know when to move and where to move, but undoubtedly he would have improved in that area from his time with Hamburg.

Andy Gray

It's all too easy to talk about Gray in terms of his bravery and his never-say-die spirit but he had much more to offer than that. Andy was a decent player with a good all-round game and while he was courageous, and would not hesitate to stick his head in where boots were flying, it was by no means the only point to his game.

You could play the ball up to Gray and he would hold it and lay it off. At the time Everton were threatening to win every trophy going and his partnership with Graeme Sharp was vital. He was great in the air and willing to run all day. Moreover he was good for team spirit, he had a presence and an enthusiasm for the game that lifted the dressing-room mood.

Andy was unlucky with injuries. Like me he had trouble with his knees but whereas I could get away with it as a central defender, for a striker it's not so easy. All the time you are having to make runs, twisting and turning and taking a buffeting from behind for your pains.

Ian Rush

When Rush first arrived at Liverpool I must confess I didn't think we had a world-beater on our hands. He was young and maybe still growing but at that time he did not show any evidence of great pace or talent.

I remember his first game at Ipswich – he was hopeless. I also recall playing with him in the reserves against Preston and telling people afterwards that I thought Liverpool were going to sell him, he was that bad. I realised long ago that a second Mystic Meg I most definitely am not! I often wonder what it was about Rushie that I missed because as an all-round striker he has been outstanding for so long.

Rest of the world forwards
1970–95

Pele

The perfect player has still to be born but Pele is the nearest we have seen so far. The Brazilian had the whole range of skills in abundance. 'Genius' and 'world-class' are terms bandied about all too readily in football but this man fits the bill – there was a freedom and a fluency about everything he did.

Pele was quick, his control was tight, he scored brilliant goals. His performance in the 1970 World Cup Final against Italy was truly magnificent.

I can't recall another player as good as him on the ground who would then be as brilliant in the air. The two don't normally go together but remember the header which opened the scoring against Italy and the one earlier in the competition from which Gordon Banks denied him with one of the outstanding saves of all time.

He was not a big man but Pele could get up well and seemed able to hang in the air for long enough to make a good connection with the ball while his defender was on the way down.

Johan Cruyff

Cruyff played for the team as well as having the individual talent to win a game on his own. He was the outstanding performer of the 1974 World Cup and while his display in the final itself disappointed, chiefly because of Berti Vogts dogged marking, his performances before then were scintillating.

Apart from his control and vision and those wonderful tricks and feints, Cruyff had greater strength than a lean frame would suggest, enabling him to shrug off defenders before laying on the killer ball. He was voted European Footballer of the Year three times.

Athletic and long-striding, Cruyff was three players in one. He could operate as the principal striker, drop deep to confuse his markers or move to the wing with devastating effect. His ability to change positions and roam around the park meant that he could also have been included in my midfield and winger categories. He fashioned crosses that were primed for his great ally, Johan Neeskens, to explode into the net.

It was on the left where he used to execute that favourite trick of his which no defender could come to terms with. With his back to goal he somehow dragged the ball behind him with his right foot, before turning away through 180 degrees, free of his man.

Maradona

Nobody wins a World Cup on their own but in 1986 Maradona came closer than most. Argentina had other capable players but without Maradona they would not have been good enough to succeed. I played against him for Scotland at Hampden when he was 18. He had a sensational talent even then and it's a shame he will be remembered for the seedier side of the game, the drug taking, instead of as a player second in ability only to Pele.

In the '86 World Cup Maradona was unstoppable, showing excellent quality as well as supreme confidence. Forget the 'Hand of God' goal – I know, it's easy for a Scot to say – but Maradona's second against England in the quarter-final was just breathtaking. Starting from his own half he took on half a team to score. Then there were his semi-final goals against Belgium. He had it all – a fantastic turn of pace, great close control, strength and a left boot packed with dynamite.

Mario Kempes

A player who is really only associated with the 1978 World Cup played in his home country, but what this tall, elegant Argentinian produced over the course of the tournament was enough to edge his way into a very competitive section. Kempes appeared to be capable of eluding all defenders. Tackles flew in and still he would calmly glide past. He was 6 ft 2 ins tall but possessed the balance of a ballet dancer.

His first touch was exemplary. That's another difference between the great and the good. The great player is not thinking about the ball as it comes, he is thinking three passes ahead, sure in the knowledge that his control will leave him with a number of options.

Kempes wasn't only a ruthless finisher, he could play 1–2s, he could do it individually, he could do it for the team; and every time he came up against the keeper it seemed the ball would end up in the back of the net.

Marco Van Basten

You could say about Van Basten, like we do with Maradona, 'What a pity it all ended the way it did.' Then again, perhaps we should be grateful we saw as much of him as we did before a major and persistent ankle injury forced him to call time on the great service he gave to AC Milan and Holland.

I remember him hitting balls from difficult positions and thinking 'why, he can't score from there', and then the next minute, there he was wheeling away, arms aloft in celebration of another fantastic strike.

The Dutchman had amazing aerial power and combined with his talent on the ground and the movement you expect from all continentals, it made him an awesome proposition for any defender.

Gerd Muller

Like all great strikers, Muller's instincts and reactions were superb. If one of his German colleagues took a shot and the goalkeeper failed to hold the ball, Muller would always be there to convert the chance.

He had enormous thighs which generated great power and made it almost impossible to knock him off the ball. His winning goal in the 1974 World Cup Final against Holland was typical – with his back to goal, one touch, a quick turn and there's the ball in the net.

Muller was an arch-predator. Put the ball in the six-yard box and he would be first to it. Nor was his short stature a handicap – he often scored with his head.

British and Irish goalscorers 1990–95

1 Gary Lineker
2 Alan Shearer
3 Ian Rush
4 Ian Wright
5 John Aldridge
6 Andy Cole

British and Irish strikers 1970–89

1 Kenny Dalglish
2 Kevin Keegan
3 Ian Rush
4 Mark Hughes
5 Graeme Sharp
6 Andy Gray

British and Irish forwards 1970–95

1 Kenny Dalglish
2 Kevin Keegan
3 Ian Rush
4 Gary Lineker
5 Alan Shearer
6 Mark Hughes

Rest of the World forwards 1970–95

1 Pele
2 Maradona
3 Johan Cruyff
4 Gerd Muller
5 Marco Van Basten
6 Mario Kempes

Super Six 1970–95

1 Pele
2 Maradona
3 Johan Cruyff
4 Gerd Muller
5 Marco Van Basten
6 Kenny Dalglish

MIDFIELD MASTERS

There are many aspects of midfield play and, domestically at least, my selection is headed by a dynamic pair who were exceptional in every area of the role. Graeme Souness and Bryan Robson were almost the complete midfield players, combining skill with aggression and determination. You couldn't argue that they possessed the artistry of a Glenn Hoddle or a Trevor Brooking but in other respects they were head and shoulders above the rest.

Hoddle and Brooking were often criticised for a lack of aggression. It was said they weren't outright winners like Souness and Robson, but when you possess that amount of talent it need not matter. Their particular strengths were such that they made up for deficiencies elsewhere.

No other classification gave me as many problems as that of the midfielders between 1970–89. It is a red-hot section, as shown by those players I had to leave out, seasoned England internationals such as Ray Wilkins, Alan Ball and Gerry Francis. Between them they gathered a huge number of international caps but I couldn't find room to fit them in.

It amazes me, too, that I cannot include Billy Bremner and Johnny Giles. Both were combative and creative and deserving of a place but in the final reckoning, amidst so much competition, I decided to stick with those whose careers were predominantly contained in the period. The Leeds pair played a lot of their football prior to 1970.

⚽   ⚽   ⚽

British and Irish midfielders
1990–95

Paul Ince

Ince's level of performance week in, week out has been as good as I've seen over the last five years. He can be niggly and cantankerous and rubs both referees and opposing fans up the wrong way, but as a midfield player with the ability to get up and down the field for 90 minutes he has no rival.

You could pull anybody off the streets and get him to work his socks off, but Ince can play as well – I honestly believe Manchester United have missed him following his transfer to Inter Milan. You cannot remove somebody who has provided that level of performance and improve things. If the object of the exercise is always to improve your side, who can you buy who's better than Ince?

He would be up to support the front men and in the next minute he would be back to protect his defence. He is not the best technical player of this six by a long way but he's quick, he tackles well and his scoring ratio is not bad.

He also works out situations and thinks about the game. Against Tottenham I saw him come up against Ilie Dumitrescu who went to go left and came in on his right. Ince was well beaten but when the Romanian tried it a second time and then again and again, Ince was waiting for him every time and was able to pick him off.

He bought the first dummy but quickly learned his lesson. Other players would have kept falling into the trap. I still see defenders coming unstuck against Chris Waddle when he does that little shuffle, feinting to hit it with his right before coming back onto his left. How can they fall for it every time? If you are beaten on the first occasion, make sure you are prepared after that.

Peter Beardsley

Beardsley is another of those who is difficult to place. Should he be in as a striker or a midfielder? In truth, he's neither, playing a lot of his football between the two areas, a real livewire who has been the scourge of defenders for years.

Peter deserves great credit for the way he has prolonged his career into his 36th year, still at the highest level and in an area of the field where it is hard for players. The onus is on the forwards to create and be inventive and, of course, up front is where the hardest knocks are handed out.

His appetite endures and that's commendable because when you've been in the game that long, it's tempting sometimes to think 'I've done enough here.' Mentally you can switch off and relax a little. The last few times I've seen him, he was as strong at the end of the game as he was at the start.

He can make goals and score goals. In my opinion he should have received a cut from the Andy Cole transfer because the wealth of chances he put Cole's way helped establish that man's £7 million reputation. Beardsley can pass the ball long or short and in tight areas his eye for a kernel of space to feed balls through to team-mates' feet is an art few others can match.

When it comes to taking chances, Peter is one of the best we have seen. He can hit them or he can dink them, he waits for the keeper to commit himself or he blasts them into the top corner. You are never sure what he's going to do and that keeps the goalkeeper guessing all the time.

On his day Beardsley is still as good as anyone in the country. If you want to pick a player to go and watch, be entertained by and to learn from, Peter is your man. A model professional who is good for a few years yet.

When he was struggling for form at Anfield, he dropped deeper and deeper and became less effective. It's why Kenny Dalglish left him out of the side. Later both Graeme Souness and Howard Kendall decided they could get along without him but at St James's Park, Beardsley has been crucial to the Newcastle revival.

It has helped that he has never taken a drink. Peter is unusual in his abstinence because most players find it the best way to relax away from the pressures of the game. When you pass 25 it is one of the things a player has to be careful of. Before then it's no problem, you can drink as much as you like, as long as you keep your glass empty towards the end of the week. But after 25 you have to take much more care of yourself, and if you look at those who go on to enjoy extended careers they have all done that. It doesn't have to be a heavy sacrifice because it's a wonderful career and there is so much to lose if you overdo things. You know as soon as you go onto the pitch or the training field what sort of physical condition you are in. If you have been over-indulging it catches you out. Even at 22 if I was having a bad run of form, I would stop drinking and take careful note of what I was eating.

Paul Gascoigne

In the end I decided I must find room for Gascoigne but I had to give it a lot of thought. We are talking about form over the last five years and to my mind he has not really reproduced the wondrous skills he showed in 1990 and '91.

He's had his bad injuries and he's still half a yard slower than he was. He's shown bits and pieces of explosive talent for Lazio, Rangers and England but they are nowhere near so commonplace as in his last two seasons with Tottenham. There hasn't been the sustained run of form.

Having said that, when Gascoigne is good he is very, very good, a sublime talent who can create goals and score goals. In his early days with Tottenham he was so strong, defenders could not shake him off the ball and it was a common sight to see him charging through three or four challenges, still retaining possession.

It's a shame what has happened to him in recent years because so much of his play in the 1990 World Cup was of star quality and you felt he could go on from there to become even better. Not that I go along with all the rave reviews his performances in Italy generated in the English press. Against Belgium for example, Gazza could not be mentioned in the same breath as Scifo, so dominant was the little Belgian, but against Cameroon he made the killer pass for Gary Lineker to take England into the semi-finals and so the legend was born.

John Barnes

There's more about Barnes in the wingers section because that is where he played his football before 1990. One of football's unanswerable questions is what is the difference between a winger and a wide midfield player? In the last couple of seasons, when he's been free of injury, John has played most of his football as a central midfielder, and with a deft touch and careful passing skills he has excelled in that position.

Gary McAllister

McAllister has a superb touch and technique. Every time I watch him play I think, what a great player. He's been unlucky in that Leeds faded from the picture a little, after winning the championship in 1992. Ince and Cantona, for example, have been involved in three championship finishes at Old Trafford and have tended to hog the spotlight.

McAllister has terrific range to his passing. He hits the ball short and long, gives it and gets it back. He gets forward well and is quick enough over the first two or three yards. Maybe he should score more goals for a midfield player but it says a lot for him that he would not have looked out of place in the great Liverpool sides.

Matt Le Tissier

People assume I don't rate Le Tissier because I've been critical of his contribution in some games, but anyone who has scored and created the number of goals that he has from a striking position or some, more often, from a slightly withdrawn role, deserves his place in the highest company. You can't argue with his talent.

My complaint is that when things aren't going so well he drifts in and out of games. I was the same – when I was having a bad time I wanted to be off and away but it's different and easier for defenders. As a creative player, Le Tissier has to be looking to receive the ball the whole time. If a Dalglish or a Shearer are not having the best of games, they will be working even harder to get it right.

Where I also think Matt is unfortunate is that because he has shown so much outlandish talent people never come away saying he had an 'all right' kind of game. He's either out of this world or he's been disappointing. In the eyes of press and public there's no in-between with Matt and it works against him.

British and Irish midfielders
1970–89

Glenn Hoddle

For absolute talent Hoddle is unrivalled, the best of the bunch. In one of Liverpool's visits to White Hart Lane, he produced over the course of 45 minutes the most outstanding display of passing I have ever witnessed. Right foot, left foot, outside of his right, inside of his left, 20 yards, 30 yards, 40, 50, no one could get near him.

I don't think I will ever see an exhibition like it again. However, to be a truly outstanding player you need more than talent and that's why Hoddle doesn't rate as number one. Too many times Spurs would come to Anfield and he would not be involved, whereas Bryan Robson, say, would be right in amongst it and not go missing. Missing is maybe not the right description but he would not be floating in and out like the Spurs man. For sheer ability, however, Hoddle had no peer.

Graeme Souness

Souness was the master. He was talented but also very strong and it's unusual to find a combination of the two.

He exuded arrogance on the pitch but it would be wrong to assume he brought that into the dressing-room. He was one of the lads and would join in all the banter, contributing very much to the team spirit.

Souness's commitment to winning was only equalled by Kenny Dalglish's and I think that's what let him down as a manager. He expected everyone to be the same but it does not work like that. For instance, I was never committed to winning like those two guys. I was sick if we lost, don't get me wrong, and sick if I hadn't played well, but winning was not the be-all and end-all. The thing that got me going was personal pride and it is essential that you are big in one of the three areas – pride, hunger and commitment.

Bryan Robson

Imagine a midfield partnership of Souness and Robson – Souness in the holding position and Robson making those dynamic charges into the opposition penalty area. Robson could attack – how many times did we see him popping up with vital goals for Manchester United and England – and he could also defend; allied to the strength of Superman, it made him an outstanding player for club and country.

Moreover, if he was having a hard time of it, he would still be in there, fighting his corner. For Robbo it was always a case of 'I'm playing for 90 minutes' and that will to win sets him apart from many of the others in this category. He had so many setbacks, injuries brought about by that never-say-die approach, but still he came back to give it his best shot. An amazing man.

Trevor Brooking

It was a toss-up between Brooking and Ray Wilkins for inclusion but Trevor is my *Match of the Day* colleague and he did name me in his book of *100 Great British Footballers*, so . . .

In the difficulties Trevor presented to defenders he reminds me of David Ginola or John Robertson. Comfortable on either foot, he didn't have to attempt to go past his opponent, one step either way would create space for the cross or the pass. Only rarely did his passes fail to find their intended target. It was said that with more aggression he would have become an even better player but that wasn't Trevor's style. He had the gift of being able to create his own time and space and maintained high standards throughout a long and distinguished career.

Liam Brady

A multi-talented, midfield artist, Brady was one of those rare players who moved from this country and found success in Italy. It's easier to go abroad and make an impression if you don't have the responsibility for scoring goals, but Brady had a head start on others with his willingness to learn and immerse himself in the Italian way of life. He had a quick brain, saw things early, and could play the big passes to his team-mates.

So if you were facing Arsenal and Brady's name was missing from the team-sheet the reaction was one of relief. Like Hoddle, when Brady was on the ball you had to get to him quickly or he might destroy you.

Terry McDermott

McDermott never received the credit he deserved for his part in Liverpool's success, probably because Souness and Dalglish claimed all the accolades. Look at the spectacular goals he scored, vital efforts like the winner in the away leg of the European Cup-tie at Aberdeen in 1980, another exquisite chip from the edge of the area against Everton in the FA Cup semi-final three years before and the header which finished off a superb end-to-end move against Spurs. The list is endless.

McDermott had a great knack of getting forward and putting the ball in the back of the net. He could run all day for you but there was so much more to his game; his touch and his passing were extra special. The esteem I hold him in is shown by the fact that I've found room for him here – the choice, maybe, that is likely to raise the most eyebrows.

Rest of the World midfielders
1970–95

Michel Platini

A midfield creator who could score fabulous goals as well, Platini was the finest footballer France has produced. For a decade he directed their midfield with a repertoire that included delicate flicks, cunning back-heels and weighted passes with the outside of either foot.

Platini continually dissected defences with passing that was inch-perfect and his free-kicks always carried the threat of a goal. He was adept at finding space in and out of the box and could be relied upon for the simple goal as well as the spectacular one.

He was outstanding in the World Cups of '82 and '86 but, despite exceptional individual performances, could not quite carry his country to the ultimate triumph. However, there was some compensation with France's victory in the 1984 European Championship on home soil. He scored in every game and was the heart and soul of a nation's footballing hopes.

Lothar Matthaus

A versatile player, Matthaus was a demanding character and stamped his personality on Germany's World Cup winning side of 1990. His two goals in the first game against Yugoslavia set a standard for the remainder of the competition.

He received the Golden Ball award as the best player of Italia '90 and followed that with prizes as the World Player of the Year, European Footballer of the Year and West German Footballer of the Year. No player has ever collected as many trophies in one year. Matthaus's great strength was running from the midfield into dangerous positions near goal. He was quick and difficult to pick up and made the most of every shooting opportunity. Power, strength and a vicious long-range shot were among his attributes. A tough competitor, his passing, touch and vision were excellent as well.

Johan Neeskens

Neeskens' contribution was often overlooked in the clamour to heap praise on Johan Cruyff but he was every bit as important to the success Holland enjoyed in the seventies. He gave them strength and skill in a vital area of the field.

His reading of the play allied to a ferocious shot helped him to score many outstanding goals, and from free-kicks and penalties he was one you could rely on to score. Without his goals in 1974, the Dutch would not have reached the World Cup Final. He excelled in all departments of the game. He could pass and move and, when the occasion demanded, he was ready to put his foot in as well.

Socrates

Socrates possessed the stamina to go from box to box for 90 minutes which proved a priceless asset for Brazil when others were wilting in the intense Spanish heat of the '82 World Cup. Yet he had a laconic, almost lazy-looking style that made you think he wasn't getting anywhere. It would lull you into a false security because when he upped the tempo he could cruise past all those in front of him in the space of only four or five strides.

Socrates was fabulous in possession and was not inclined to waste it, his brilliant passing skills often tearing defences to shreds. He could operate in a free role on the right or in the centre of midfield; wherever he was detailed to play he would need a lot of watching.

Paul Breitner

Breitner could perform both the midfield roles – defensive or attacking – and, with a confidence bordering on arrogance, could control the game by allowing the star player on the other side little chance to shine.

Breitner's versatility was such that he could play in all three positions – defence, midfield and attack. He was a vital player, crucial to the success of Bayern Munich in the 1970s and of West Germany in the 1974 World Cup, but someone who could never be classed as a team player. Apparently he was the last to arrive for training and the first to leave and it was said that he was so keen to escape from his team-mates that he used to leave the training ground with his hair still wet.

Still, his colleagues were able to forgive his non-conformist ways when he produced his match-winning performances and outstanding goals, struck from outside the box. Elsewhere, pass and move was his philosophy. The formidable combination of his touch and technical ability along with mental strength and cast-iron determination has never been more obvious on the world stage.

Gerson

Looks can be deceiving. At first glance Gerson, rounded and languid-looking, didn't give the impression that he was a mobile midfield player and in truth he seemed to play at his own pace.

Give the Brazilian the ball, however, and he could make it do wondrous things. His eye for the pass was exceptional.

He had a disappointing World Cup in 1966 but he learned from the experience and returned four years later to play a starring role in Mexico. It certainly came as a surprise to his former club, Botafogo, who had allowed him to move to Sao Paulo in 1969, believing his best days to be in the past.

In the 1970 World Cup Gerson, in a team of stars, was very often the man to make things happen. Granted space to play, he could make it count. A superb left foot laid on goalscoring chances for his team and in the final he deservedly put himself on the scoresheet with an emphatic low drive from outside the penalty area giving Brazil a 2–1 lead over the Italians.

British and Irish midfielders 1990–95

1 Paul Ince
2 Peter Beardsley
3 John Barnes
4 Paul Gascoigne
5 Matt Le Tissier
6 Gary McAllister

British and Irish midfielders 1970–89

1 Graeme Souness
2 Bryan Robson
3 Glenn Hoddle

4 Liam Brady
5 Terry McDermott
6 Trevor Brooking

British and Irish midfielders 1970–95

1 Graeme Souness
2 Bryan Robson
3 Glenn Hoddle
4 Liam Brady
5 Terry McDermott
6 Trevor Brooking

Rest of the World midfielders 1970–95

1 Michel Platini
2 Gerson
3 Johan Neeskens
4 Paul Breitner
5 Socrates
6 Lothar Matthaus

Super Six 1970–95

1 Michel Platini
2 Gerson
3 Johan Neeskens
4 Graeme Souness
5 Bryan Robson
6 Paul Breitner

Ball-Winners

Not so long ago, no side would be without a midfield enforcer, a strong tackler who could break up opposing attacks and put his own team back in possession. At Liverpool in the second half of the eighties and early nineties, we included two ball-winners in Ronnie Whelan and Steve McMahon but the great thing was that they could both play as well. Like Graeme Souness and Jimmy Case who also functioned together superbly in the same side, they were ball-winners but also ball-users.

There is a fashion now to dispense with the traditional ball-winner. England had been using Paul Ince in the withdrawn midfield role but, in 1995, Terry Venables decided he could get by without an out-and-out ball-winner and Ince was left out.

Liverpool have done something similar, preferring to employ two players comfortable on the ball – John Barnes and Jamie Redknapp – with Steve McManaman left free to run with it and create space for the strikers. In the Liverpool system of a five-man defence, where you defend deep and pull men behind the ball, a tackler is not absolutely vital. In my day, we used a flat back four, defended further up the field, and in those circumstances it's necessary to employ someone in front to break things up.

Venables has clearly decided England are good enough in possession to do without a player to win the ball back for them. I find it hard to agree. To my mind, Ince has stood head and shoulders above any other midfield player in the last three years and England have missed him, or a player of his type.

The proviso I have made when making my selection is that ball-winners have to be able to use the ball successfully. Merely winning back possession is not enough on its own.

Steve McMahon and Ronnie Whelan

Both McMahon and Whelan can consider themselves unfortunate not to have won a place in the midfield category. Their contribution for Liverpool from 1986 onwards was such that they could have walked into any side in the country. Graeme Souness was the outstanding performer in the role but these two ran him very close.

They were the dream ticket – they could win the ball, and then make good use of it themselves. Their presence in the Liverpool side of the late eighties and early nineties was vital when we had flair players of the calibre of John Barnes, Ray Houghton and Peter Beardsley. In a set-up like that you also need players who can rough it when the situation demands.

Whelan was one of those unlucky players who the fans didn't appreciate until he was out of the side. He picked up a lot of injuries towards the end of his career and after 1990 faded out of the picture but people forgot he was a big-time player at Liverpool for a long, long while. He got into the team when he was 19, and appeared in over 500 games.

He didn't exude the tough-man image that others in this list have, but he was hard and resolute. He was an intelligent player and knew how to time his tackles. His injuries weren't as a result of tackling wildly.

Billy Bremner

He had a short, squat frame and some said he had the face of a schoolboy but, boy, could Bremner compete. With a terrific engine and a big heart, he seemed to cover most of the midfield area and with his scurrying combativeness he was a perfect foil for the passing ability and control of Johnny Giles. He was aggressive and fiery and that frequently got him into trouble with referees and opponents.

Bremner tackled crisply and effectively and, having won the ball, he could set up attacks with a quick pass. He and Giles rarely gave the ball away and their Leeds United side were one of the first to perfect the possession game.

Bryan Robson

When at the height of his powers, and not suffering from another in a long list of injuries, Robson was not only one of the strongest tacklers but also one of the most athletic players. His appetite for the game, his willingness to compete and fight for every ball made him a player that every manager would want in their side. He was a non-stop performer, tackling, working back and covering as well as any back-four player.

Billy Bonds

You never tackled Bonds without thinking that you had run into something really solid. It was like taking on a brick wall, even though his tackles were always 100 per cent legitimate. West Ham came to Anfield near the end of Bonds' career when he must have been about 39 but the feeling was still the same – you tackled him and it hurt.

He was another, though, who gained a hard-man reputation and it tended to overshadow his other qualities. For instance he was superb at locating his team-mates with passes hit off either foot. He operated as Trevor Brooking's 'minder' for many seasons in midfield and later went back to perform as an outstanding centre-back, having begun his career in the number two shirt.

Graeme Souness

Souness could play in any of the midfield positions. He was more than useful in an advanced role but it was in that withdrawn area, protecting his back four, sticking his foot in and occasionally driving forward, that he was a player apart.

Once he had won the ball, Graeme showed what tremendous variety he had in his game. He could pass it long or short. To add to that he scored plenty of goals, he hit them from 25 yards and they flew in. When he was at his best the whole show flowed from him. He had presence and star quality.

Since 1990, apart from Ince, David Howells has impressed as a ball-winner, employed by Tottenham to boss the area between midfield and defence and to stabilise a side that was leaking too many goals. The transformation was immediate. David Batty has used his aggressive tendencies to good effect for both Leeds and Blackburn, and when Paul McGrath was selected in the role for the Republic of Ireland there were few who could have done it better.

British and Irish ball-winners 1970–95

1 Graeme Souness
2 Bryan Robson
3 Billy Bremner
4 Billy Bonds
5 Steve McMahon and Ronnie Whelan

GREAT GOALKEEPERS

The secret of good goalkeeping is to keep out goals! To do that it helps to be an organiser and a good communicator. Ray Clemence was ideal for me when I first came into the Liverpool side. He would call out 'one yard to the left' or 'two to the right' and make sure I was in the best position to react to danger.

A decisive keeper is a boon to any defence. There is nothing worse for a centre-back if a cross is launched into the middle and you are unsure whether the man behind you is coming to take it or whether you must deal with it yourself.

The calibre of British keepers before 1990 was outstanding. No other country produced candidates to match them and the big four – Gordon Banks, Peter Shilton, Pat Jennings and Ray Clemence – occupy the same positions in my overall category. They set standards no one else could reach and were responsible for their teams winning many fixtures. It was a good era; dependable characters like Joe Corrigan at Manchester City are unlucky to miss out.

British and Irish goalkeepers
1990–95

David Seaman

Seaman was the last line of a defence which conceded only 18 goals in Arsenal's championship season of 1990–91. For a goalkeeper, however good your outfield players are, however disciplined and miserly are the defence, a statistic like that says everything about your ability to keep the ball out of the net.

David looks big in the goal and gives the impression of being hard to beat although he would probably admit to a flaw when facing shots from 60 yards in a European final! His performances for Arsenal have been remarkably consistent but even before he went to Highbury his contribution to QPR was such that he came close to a place on the 1970–89 list. Over the last five years he is undisputably number one.

Tim Flowers

Tim Flowers has had his critics and his red-faced moments but he was brilliant when it mattered in the climax to the 1995 championship. When Blackburn played Newcastle towards the end of their chase with Manchester United, Kevin Keegan's side posed them a mighty challenge. The win was vital for Rovers and, as they were put under immense pressure and their lead came under serious threat, Flowers was inspirational.

For a large man he is extremely agile. He bosses his area well and is a good organiser. He makes sure defenders know exactly what he wants.

Bruce Grobbelaar

I would never tell anybody to study Grobbelaar's style of goal-keeping. He is a one-off but so very effective. I think he has been unlucky – because of the fact that he comes for everything his mistakes are highlighted, especially in these days of wall-to-wall television.

For those keepers who stay on the line, mistakes are never going to be so transparent. If you are coming for everything it's an absolute certainty that you won't collect everything and when the ball's in the back of the net people will obviously start pointing fingers at the man in goal.

If a keeper relies on defenders to knock centres away, the law of averages says eventually he will come unstuck. It is much better for the keeper to come and use his height advantage. It does not matter how good the centre-forward is in the air, the keeper will win every time or, at least, he should do. If the keeper leaves it to the defence, there's only a 50 per cent chance that the centre-half will win the ball and clear the danger.

Moreover, with Grobbelaar collecting the cross, the ball is immediately back in his team's possession, whereas an outfield player's defensive clearance could end up anywhere. Liverpool's success was founded on retaining possession.

Chris Woods

Woods has been a leading goalkeeper for a very long time but he has been unlucky with injuries and has struggled to put his career back on track.

Woods deputised superbly for Peter Shilton in his early days at Nottingham Forest and was responsible for holding Liverpool up in the 1978 League Cup Final. For someone to come into a big occasion like that, young and inexperienced, and yet perform so well spoke volumes for his temperament and nerve. Shots and crosses – he showed he could deal admirably with both.

He waited a long while to take over from Shilton in the England set-up and was unfortunate not to have had a longer run in the side. He picked up injuries, lost confidence and then David Seaman arrived to stake his claim. The same happened at Sheffield Wednesday where Kevin Pressman came in and did so well that Woods couldn't win back his place.

Neville Southall

Southall excels at one-on-ones and, in an illustrious career with Everton, has pulled off reaction saves that defied belief. His anticipation is sharp and he regularly shows great courage by diving headlong into a mass of flailing boots to retrieve the ball.

In his later years, Southall has been beaten by shots from 25 yards that you think he should have saved. He makes up for it with his reflex stops from close in, but it has led to the obituary-writers penning a premature end to his career.

In my view he was helped by Joe Royle's arrival at Goodison. When Mike Walker departed, the team were so out of sorts that five or six looked as if they had never been players. Royle managed to put the smile back on their faces and convince all the players of their ability. He did wonders for Southall who was outstanding in all the rounds as Everton won their way through to the FA Cup Final. He capped it off with his performance at Wembley, the saves he pulled off there showed that, on his day, he is still among the very best.

Andy Goram

The Rangers man has done exceedingly well for his club. He's not the biggest man in this category, and while he's OK on crosses, his best work is in dealing with shots. His shot-stopping techniques are superb.

Goram joined the Ibrox club at a time when Chris Woods had the jersey and was performing well. The fact that Walter Smith thought Goram a better bet for his team shows how highly he was rated at that time. Since then he has confirmed that promise and gone on to become Scotland's number one.

British and Irish goalkeepers
1970–89

Gordon Banks

Banks never took risks. He played by percentages and made the art of goalkeeping look so easy. Cool under pressure, he was a natural with fantastic positional sense, tremendous agility and strong reflexes.

Through years of specialised training, Banks emerged as the man every team wanted behind them. In the build-up to the World Cup finals in 1966 he kept three clean sheets, adding another three in the opening games. Imagine the confidence that gives a defence. You believe your keeper to be unbeatable.

Banks was magnificent in 1966 but everyone will remember him for the save from Pele in the 1970 World Cup finals against Brazil. He was still scurrying across his goal-line as the great man applied, with force, a downward header that was destined for the bottom corner of the net. Somehow Banks got down, twisted his body and scooped the ball to safety.

Peter Shilton

Shilton always seemed to save his best performances for when he was facing Liverpool. We went through a spell when we could not find a way past him and as a result Nottingham Forest had the Indian sign over us.

They thoroughly deserved their two European Cup triumphs but in those days Forest were light years behind Liverpool both as a team and in individual skill. Yet they had Shilts in goal and that counted for so much.

If he had a weakness it was on crosses. We would try to tempt him off his line and then pile bodies in on him because we thought we could get him that way. Yet compared to his strengths on the goal-line, it was a minute disadvantage. In one-on-one situations he is the best I have ever seen; he stood up for as long as it mattered and put all the onus on the attacking player to find a way to beat him.

Shilton's shot-stopping was the cornerstone of his success. His reflexes were such that he could get to anything. He was an inspirational role model for aspiring keepers. His dedication to his craft was incredible, his hatred for conceding goals legendary. His chastening of his defenders when a shot had slipped through was comical at times but, to be fair, he was equally hard on himself when he thought he had not lived up to his own towering standards.

Bruce Grobbelaar

It makes me smile when I hear people say Grobbelaar was the weak link in the Liverpool side, that he gave away too many goals. He would not have played for Liverpool for as long as he did and picked up that many medals if he was not a top-rate operator. You win nothing with bad players, least of all with a bad goalkeeper. It is the most crucial position on the pitch and it is impossible to have continued success with a bad 'un, no matter how good the other ten players are.

Talk to all his team-mates and all the managers he played under and the verdict would be unanimous: Bruce was one of the best. If he hadn't been, he would have been out on his ear, it's as simple as that.

Of course there were goals he gave away but what goalkeeper can say they haven't been embarrassed by one or two? Bruce was brilliant for the defenders in front of him because he would always come for crosses. Sometimes that let him down if his judgement was a fraction awry but for the occasional mistake you could reckon on him saving many more by coming so far to collect the ball.

Ray Clemence

They told me that in his early days at Liverpool Clemence would come for everything. He had a terrific spring and secure hands yet when I was playing he came for nothing. Either way as a defender you don't mind; the important thing is to know who's doing what.

Ray had a slighter build and was probably more athletic than Shilton. His agility helped him get to shots you felt were beyond reach. From both their points of view, it was a shame that he and Shilton were around at the same time because either could have gone on to break Pat Jennings's record of 119 international caps. When Ron Greenwood was the England manager he said he could not judge between them and they were forced to share the honour with alternate appearances, a situation that suited nobody.

Ray had a flawless eye for spotting danger and carried on the example set by his Liverpool predecessor, Tommy Lawrence, who was the first to widen goalkeeping responsibilities so that keepers became virtual sweepers behind the back four. Ray patrolled the edge of his area with great assurance and would often sprint yards out of his box to boot the ball away.

Neville Southall

Southall was the backbone behind Everton's success in the 1980s. In their championship seasons of '85 and '87 he frequently produced saves that proved to be the turning point in crucial games.

In 1985 he was inspirational as Everton pursued the treble and added the Cup Winners' Cup to the league title. One stop from Mark Falco in a game that effectively ended Tottenham's challenge recalled memories of Banks's great plunging save to deny Pele's header. His colleagues were not surprised; according to them Southall was making saves like that every week.

Pat Jennings

There have been few players in any position who were so admired for so long as Jennings. As an all-round keeper he was as good as they come. On his line, off his line, you could barely discern a fault in his make-up. With guys like Shilton, Clemence or Jennings behind them, defenders start with a distinct advantage. The confidence spreads throughout the team. You know that if you make a mistake there's someone behind who will save you from embarrassment whereas if you are playing in front of a dodgy keeper, it's easy to feel edgy yourself.

Jennings exuded confidence. His particular trademark was coming from his line and picking off crosses one-handed – his hands were so big it was almost an unfair advantage. Very rarely did you see Pat come for a ball and not win it. His anticipation and reading of the flight of a cross were exceptional. He also became adept at stopping shots with his legs and his feet.

Rest of the World goalkeepers
1970–95

Sepp Maier

The West German was a funny man. He dressed funny and acted funny but his record as a top goalkeeper was less than funny as far as opposing strikers were concerned.

Maier was a gambler in goalkeeping terms and more often than not the gamble paid off. He was strong in the air, quick-thinking and positive. In the World Cup in Mexico in 1970 he was not totally convincing and was dropped. But he recovered his form to win his place back for the 1974 finals in his home country.

He performed consistently well throughout the tournament but in the final against the Dutch he excelled himself, exuding calm assurance and complete control when others might have fallen apart.

Dino Zoff

They say goalkeepers can go on for ever but to captain your country in the World Cup Final at the age of 40 is a remarkable achievement. Zoff was fond of establishing records. At club level he went 903 minutes without conceding a goal and for Italy did even better, holding out with his goal intact for an incredible 1,143 minutes.

Zoff's great strengths were his total command of his area, his ability as a shot-stopper and the ease with which he dealt with crosses. That's one area of the continental keeper's make-up that, at Liverpool, we always thought we had a chance to exploit. In European ties we would encourage our wide men to put over a stream of high balls from the flanks.

Zoff played in three World Cup finals. In the last one in Spain, in 1982, he confounded those experts who were writing him off by going on to lift the trophy. He made crucial stops all the way through, especially against Argentina and Brazil in a heavyweight second-round stage. Brazil only needed a draw to progress to the semi-finals but found Zoff at his inspirational best, producing save after vital save.

Peter Schmeichel

Schmeichel has everything a top goalkeeper needs but like others mentioned he has a weakness when it comes to fielding crosses. Having said that, when he does leave his line and gathers the ball cleanly, his ability to turn defence into attack with a launch of one of his long throws is second to none.

He has stopped some shots when the attacker has already turned away in celebration of a goal. He just seems to stretch himself those vital few inches to get his fingers to the ball.

Renat Dasayev

The Soviet Union produced one of the all-time great goalkeepers in the legendary Lev Yashin and the man who shone for his country in the 1982 and '86 World Cups was a worthy successor. Dasayev's selection for the Rest of the World side who played in the Football League centenary match at Wembley in 1987 underlined how highly he was rated. A very capable keeper, who made few mistakes, he was the pick of the bunch in Spain in 1982.

Claudio Taffarel

The Brazilians are hardly renowned for producing outstanding goalkeepers but Taffarel showed in the 1994 USA World Cup that he knew his job. Others captured the glory but he made a crucial contribution to his country's tournament victory.

Solid and capable, he conceded only three goals in the whole competition – two of which came in the quarter-final against Holland – underlining the emphasis that these South Americans were happy to place on sound, responsible defending. They had flair and expertise in attack – though comparisons with the 1970 Brazilians just do not stand up – but made sure it was not at the expense of other areas of the team.

Harald Schumacher

I am reluctant to name the West German in this company because his brutal attack on Patrick Battison in the World Cup semi-final in Spain in 1982 remains one of football's most horrific images. Having removed that from my chest, it has also to be acknowledged that Schumacher was a highly capable keeper and a difficult man to beat.

British and Irish keepers 1990–95

1 David Seaman
2 Tim Flowers
3 Bruce Grobbelaar
4 Chris Woods
5 Neville Southall
6 Andy Goram

British and Irish keepers 1970–89

1 Gordon Banks
2 Peter Shilton
3 Pat Jennings
4 Ray Clemence
5 Bruce Grobbelaar
6 Neville Southall

British and Irish keepers 1970–95

1 Gordon Banks
2 Peter Shilton
3 Pat Jennings
4 Ray Clemence
5 Bruce Grobbelaar
6 Neville Southall

Rest of the World keepers 1970–95

1 Dino Zoff
2 Sepp Maier
3 Peter Schmeichel
4 Renat Dasayev

5 Claudio Taffarel
6 Harald Schumacher

Super Six 1970–95

1 Gordon Banks
2 Peter Shilton
3 Pat Jennings
4 Ray Clemence
5 Bruce Grobbelaar
6 Neville Southall

Goalkeeper Blunders

Rene Higuita

The eccentric Colombian goalkeeper executed the bizarre scorpion kick at Wembley in 1995 which emphasised his reputation as someone with a penchant for the unorthodox. However, his countrymen weren't laughing along with his eccentricity at the 1990 World Cup when he was responsible for Colombia's second-round exit at the hands of Cameroon.

With the game in extra time, out came Higuita from his goal on another upfield sortie. He tried to dribble around the Cameroon forward Roger Milla and came unstuck, left stranded as Milla took the ball off him to score. It was a crazy gamble which failed and cost his team the game.

Bruce Grobbelaar

Grobbelaar did something similar when Liverpool faced Sheffield Wednesday at Anfield in September 1984. Stranded outside the 18-yard box he attempted to dribble around Imre Varadi and showed absolutely no touch or control. I always reminded him of it when he used to say he was so talented he could comfortably play centre-half.

In the dressing-room afterwards we all went crazy at him. He held up his hands and admitted the mistake but wanted to know where the rest of us were at the crucial moment. My reply was that we could have been Carl Lewis times two and still would not have been quick enough to get back and retrieve the mistake.

Stewart Kennedy

Kennedy was the unlucky goalkeeper for Scotland on the day England hammered the auld enemy at Wembley in 1975. The score finished 5–1 and Kennedy seemed to be diving everywhere except near the ball.

For a Scottish supporter the goals were nothing short of tragic but hindsight lends them a comical edge. The Rangers man always seemed to be starting his dive just as the ball struck the back of the net. Colin Bell hit one and I can still see Kennedy diving in slow motion. Kevin Beattie scored with his head from about 20 yards and somehow Kennedy ended up hanging from the bar. It was comic cut stuff.

Alan Rough

Scotland played Russia in Malaga needing a win to go through to the next group stage in the 1982 World Cup. It did not help matters when Willie Miller and I collided in the centre of the pitch allowing Chivadze a free run on goal although Alan Rough's effort at going down at his feet was probably the worst I have ever seen. Talk about going down in instalments – it must have taken him a good five minutes to hit the deck.

Ray Clemence

When Clemence was playing for England against Scotland at Hampden in 1976 he let in an easy one against Kenny Dalglish which guaranteed him unmerciful stick from the Liverpool dressing-room for a long time after.

It was the softest of soft goals and a real howler for such an excellent keeper, especially in the context of an England–Scotland clash. Dalglish was under pressure as he prepared to shoot and could not apply much power to the ball but it ended up trickling through Clem's legs. Sheer bliss for every Scotsman; especially as Scotland went on to win the game 2–1.

Gary Sprake

On a celebrated occasion at Anfield, Sprake threw the ball into his own goal. Immediately the Kop responded with a chorus of 'Careless Hands'. It was not the only occasion when the Leeds keeper dropped a clanger. At Wembley in 1970, Sprake was left embarrassed when he allowed a long shot from Peter Houseman, and not a particularly fierce shot at that, to squirm under his dive and present Chelsea with their first equaliser in an FA Cup Final that eventually went to a replay and victory for the London club.

IT'S A FUNNY OLD GAME

There were always plenty of laughs with Liverpool, both at the training ground and at Anfield: the mickey-taking that went on in the dressing-room could be ruthless. Normally it would be the three Scots – myself, Graeme Souness and Kenny Dalglish – dishing it out. We loved to be in the middle of the fun but were not so keen to be on the receiving end.

The lads who came to the club in my later years described it as a three-month initiation course they had to overcome. John Aldridge for example was absolutely slaughtered for his goalscoring record with Ireland which at that time was abysmal. It was all done in fun. If the target for our ribbing could not handle it, we would stop. Aldo could see the funny side of it and would retaliate in turn.

Managers and coaches would all join in with the banter. It was an ideal way to bring some light relief to the dressing-room. Then twenty minutes before kick-off the joking would stop and the serious business would begin.

Steve Nicol

The minute Nicol came into a room he brightened the scene for everyone. He was a brilliant mimic and very sharp in his observations.

Nicol was superb at taking off the archetypal Scottish supporter, the fickle Hampden fan who quickly changes from 'Come on

Scotland, I love you Scotland', to 'That's a load of rubbish Scotland', and then to 'I'll nae be back Scotland'.

There was one time when we had gone to play an exhibition match in Dubai. On the way home we were diverted to Bahrain and went inside the airport for lunch. After a while Steve tried to leave the room but the walls were made up of glass panels and he couldn't find the door. That was funny in itself because he really exaggerated his predicament. But he took it a stage further. In the corner of the room was a lectern and in front of 600 people, who didn't have a clue who he was, he began to deliver a sermon. It was a sensational performance.

Alan Irvine

A big Scottish centre-forward who had come to Liverpool from Falkirk, Irvine fancied himself as a bit of a pop star and he had the patter to go with it. He was a funny guy to have around and seemed to have a never-ending supply of gags.

He had not long arrived at the club when we were due to play an FA Cup replay against Luton. Before a home game we used to gather at the Holiday Inn for our match preparations. It so happened that that was where Alan and his family were staying.

At five o'clock Roy Evans came up to the fifth floor where we had been having our afternoon nap with the message that the coach would leave for the ground at ten to six. At that point Alan went down to his family room on the third floor and so was not around when Roy reappeared ten minutes later to tell us the game was off; Luton could not get out of Heathrow because of fog.

Half the players had their cars at the hotel and immediately set off home. The rest were parked at Anfield so at ten to six, still in our tracksuits, we boarded the coach to go back to the ground. Alan came out in his jacket and tie, dressed for the game. Immediately I realised that he had missed Roy's second message and was blissfully unaware that the game had been called off.

I suggested to Kenny Dalglish that we should kid him along that he was about to make his debut. There were only seven of us seated on the bus but Alan didn't cotton on that something was amiss.

Kenny had a word, informed Alan he was playing, and ordered him to keep it to himself. Of course, the rest of us knew what was going on and pressed Alan to let on. Eventually he succumbed.

When we arrived at Anfield it was a perfect scenario; because the game was called off late there were lots of fans still milling around. We got to the dressing-room and Kenny kept the joke going by laying out the team board and the counters and telling Alan that he was playing just off the front two. He moved the counters around and gave Alan his instructions. Still he didn't suss what was going on, even though there were only seven of us in the dressing-room and only seven counters on the table.

Eventually Alan went out into reception and asked Fred, who used to look after the dressing-room, where he should leave the match tickets for his family to pick up. Fred gave him a strange look and said: 'But the game was called off at five o'clock!' They accuse Dalglish of lacking humour but the way he managed to keep the gag going put the lie to that.

Ronnie Rosenthal

In international weeks, when so many senior players were away with their countries, we used to finish a training session at Melwood with a game which involved everyone, senior players, reserves and the youth team. It was something like 16-a-side!

The first time Ronnie Rosenthal was around on one of these occasions, he came up to me as the game was starting and asked what was going on. I said it was the big game, Ronnie, with different rules. I explained that you scored one goal by putting the ball in the back of the net but three if you took the ball over the by-line and sat on it. Of course it was a wind-up but he went for it hook, line and sinker.

We were about thirty seconds into the game when Rosenthal got possession. He ran past Ronnie Moran on the left-hand side, over the by-line and proceeded to sit on the ball looking ever so pleased with himself. Moran looked him up and down as though he'd taken leave of his senses. It was a priceless moment.

Bruce Grobbelaar

Probably the most extrovert character I have ever met, Grobbelaar lived life and played other sports the way he did his football – everything was Hollywood. If he was playing snooker he wouldn't know the meaning of a safety shot, if it was golf every ball was there to be smashed out of sight.

Bruce would talk about anything and everything. Bring up any subject and he would give you a twenty-minute dissertation. If you said you went to the moon yesterday he would say he had been there the previous Thursday. An amazing man and fantastic value in the dressing-room. His bizarre 'wobbly-legs' cameo to distract the Roma penalty-taker in the 1984 European Cup Final was typical Bruce. I had not seen that particular routine before, nor since. It was something he just decided to do on the spur of the moment and it worked for him.

Terry McDermott

McDermott was brilliant at taking off Bob Paisley. While my first Liverpool manager was absolutely spot on with the things he said, he had trouble getting his message over. He was not a great talker and sometimes he would tie himself in knots – and us as well.

When Bob was in charge we used to have a team meeting every Friday morning. It was the highlight of the week. Before he came in, Terry would get all the players round and give the speech. He had him off to a tee. When Paisley came into the room the big test was to keep a straight face because Terry had predicted exactly what the manager was going to say.

There was a time when we were going through a bad patch and no one was scoring. We went six or seven games without a goal and invariably Terry Mac would be the one to make way for the substitute in the second half. We used to say he was the victim of the pop-up toaster: up would pop his number on the board on the touchline and off he would go.

After a few games and still no goals, Terry was left out of the team at Coventry. Before the kick-off while the rest of us were getting changed, he was in the dressing-room skimming through

Gary Lineker's exceptional pace made him a scourge for every defender. Scotland's Alex McLeish is left helpless as he shoots for goal.

Not the complete player, but no one can overlook Matt Le Tissier's wonderful skills both as a creator of goals and as a finisher.

Johan Cruyff deserved to be a World Cup winner and when he earned this first-minute penalty in the 1974 final against West Germany he looked to be on the way.

Mark Hughes, one of the best at holding the ball and bringing others into play, prevents West Ham's Steve Potts from making his tackle.

Michel Platini, number one in the midfield category, receiving the 1984
European Championship trophy.

His record at Newcastle was phenomenal but Andy Cole could score even more if he took a tip from Peter Beardsley and varied his shots.

Peter Beardsley has been a superb player for many years and could have won a place in two categories: strikers and midfielders.

Gordon Strachan just keeps going and going, a marvellous competitor and an outstanding winger.

Bruce Grobbelaar was brilliant for the defenders in front of him even though his habit of coming for every cross left me with a sore head on occasions!

Diego Maradona scored great goals all the way through the 1986 World Cup
finals and was a worthy winning captain.

The 1995 championship decider at West Ham: Manchester United manager Alex Ferguson signals Blackburn's score at Liverpool but his team couldn't quite pull it off.

Franz Beckenbauer – an outstanding manager and before that the best central defender there has ever been.

Others like Bob Paisley won more trophies but for me Bill Shankly was the greatest manager because of the dynasty he created at Liverpool.

For sheer ability there was no better midfielder than Glenn Hoddle. Here he weighs up another defence-splitting pass.

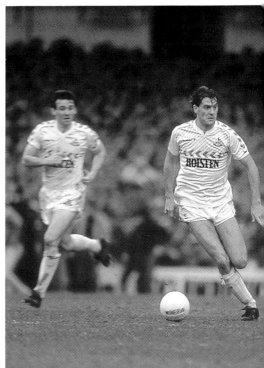

Ian Rush has had an incredible career for club and country – to think that when he first arrived at Anfield I did not rate him!

Neville Southall: a great goalkeeper in both the 80's and 90's. His career was revived when Joe Royle took over at Everton.

Gordon Banks made countless magnificent saves but even he could not get to everything. Tottenham twice found a way past him in the 1961 FA Cup final with Leicester.
George Best strikes for goal – I am just glad I never had to find a way to stop him.

the programme. He found the crossword page. 'Look at this clue,' he said, 'Liverpool striker, four letters. The answer's easy – none.' With that he turned and walked out of the dressing-room, leaving the rest of us in fits.

Phil Thompson

The 1981 European Cup Final in Paris against Real Madrid was staged at the Parc des Princes, a rugby ground, and there was something wrong with the pitch markings that night. Every time the ball hit the white lines it bounced all over the place.

There were ten minutes left in the game when the ball passed over my head. Behind me, in a covering position as usual, was Phil Thompson while Graeme Souness was also converging in case of danger.

The ball hit the penalty-area line and shot up wildly, smacking Thommo flush on the nose and he did have a hooter to be proud of! For the next five minutes Souness and I couldn't play for laughing which just shows that even on the biggest occasions there can be room for a smile.

CLASSY CENTRAL DEFENDERS

If a central defender has a poor appreciation of positional play, if he goes missing from vital areas at crucial times, he is a liability to his team. First and foremost, an understanding of the right positions to take up is the asset a central defender must have, yet that and an ability to read the game are both difficult aspects to coach.

You hear people extolling the virtues of pace and how it will help retrieve a mistake if you've been caught in the wrong position. The flaw in that argument is that eventually you will come up against someone just as quick. Then if you are caught on the wrong side you will be left for dead.

A great example came at Wembley in 1993 when Des Walker was embarrassed by Marc Overmars and conceded the penalty for Holland's equaliser which went a long way towards ensuring that England did not qualify for the USA World Cup. A less speedy opponent and Walker would have retrieved his poor positioning and saved the day.

With other attributes, a lack of pace can be camouflaged. Bobby Moore and Phil Thompson rate one and two on my list for the earlier era, and neither was blessed with speed; nor were Terry Butcher and Norman Hunter, terrific defenders who would guard their territory with fortitude and strength. However, I could not quite squeeze them into the list.

British and Irish central defenders
1990–95

Gary Pallister

Pallister impresses me every time I see him. Individually his performances have been outstanding and his Manchester United partnership with Steve Bruce is unsurpassed over the last few years.

When he first signed for United, Gary's positional play let him down. There seemed to be a problem with his understanding with Bruce and he was finding himself in some of the worst positions I have seen. But throughout the last four seasons he and the United skipper have been crucial to the club's success and have shone as a partnership. This is what centre-back play should be like. The two men in the middle have to be working in tandem, pushing and pulling the full-backs in and out of position.

The minute United come under pressure, more often than not it is Pallister to the rescue. Absolutely brilliant in the air, he tackles well and he is quick.

Paul McGrath

Had we been analysing performances between 1983–88, McGrath would have come out top of the class and it is a tribute to him and his durability that he still warrants inclusion after 1990 when his career has been winding down. Mind you, how long have we been saying that he is approaching the final whistle – and still he carries on strong.

To perform as he has done for Aston Villa and the Republic of Ireland without the benefit of daily training is a feat in itself. His injured knees prevent him from doing anything apart from playing the games and yet he still maintains exceedingly high standards.

McGrath uses his experience well and his vision means that he can spot danger well in advance. His brain is as sharp as ever and helps cut down the miles he has to travel on a football field. Superb in the air, he is also a sound tackler.

It's been said that Manchester United got rid of him too early. There is some truth in that but the counter-argument is that if they hadn't produced the defensive vacancy they would not have been able to bring together Bruce and Pallister.

Tony Adams

Adams has improved dramatically as an all-round footballer. He's always had a big heart, a dominating presence in the air and been prepared to give 110 per cent to the team; but in other respects his game has taken on a new dimension. He knows when to tackle and when not to tackle, when to shepherd opponents into areas where you want them and when to put his foot in.

He and Pallister are England's best and as a combination they dovetail well. Apart from Newcastle's Steve Howey, I don't see anyone challenging them closely, though when they play together they have to be careful not to be caught square. Pallister is quick whereas Adams lacks speed on the turn and must always be wary of leaving too much space between him and the goalkeeper.

Steve Bruce

When you look at centre-backs in this country there aren't too many who use the ball effectively. Bruce plays it simple and in many ways that is a plus. The Manchester United stalwart has learned the centre-back role and learned very well.

He began his professional career as a midfield player and has used that experience to his advantage. Another whose shortage of pace never seems to find him out, few strikers over the last few years have had the satisfaction of mastering him.

Colin Hendry

I joined Kenny Dalglish on a scouting expedition to watch Hendry when he was with Blackburn first time round, before his move to Manchester City. At that time he was a useful stopper but he would not have been the right purchase for Liverpool because he could not pass the ball.

At Anfield they have always liked defenders who could play it out from the back. Yet with the all-round improvement in Colin's game over the last two or three years, I now believe he could play for any team in the country. He passes all the tests but primarily he's a superb tackler, brave and frequently throwing his body into challenges.

The Blackburn way of playing suits him. They soak up pressure and defend the 18-yard line and that's ideal for defenders who are good in the air. In this country, teams aren't clever enough to pass through you. Eventually they have to knock the ball in the air, allowing the tall defenders to stand there and lap it up.

In all my years at Liverpool we defended the 18-yard line just twice, both times on the plastic at Luton. If the ball was knocked behind you on that surface there was no way of recovering. I came away each time wishing we could play that way every week because it is so much easier, especially for those guys who *are* good in the air and I wasn't particularly strong in that department. It is when a defender gets dragged up the pitch that his problems occur.

Des Walker

Walker has never been great positionally and I always felt that as soon as he lost his burning pace he would find himself exposed more and more. I saw him caught on the wrong side too many times, only recovering through a terrific turn of foot.

The problem was that as soon as he came up against someone just as quick, he would be unable to bring those recovery skills into play and that's how Overmars was able to show him up at Wembley.

Having said that, Des has done well to recapture his form with Sheffield Wednesday because he had a bad run with England and then had a disappointing experience in Italy. The level of performance he was producing for his country early in his career was of such a high standard that people considered him bomb-proof. As soon as someone is thought incapable of a poor game it tends to make his mistakes, rare though they are, more glaring.

British and Irish central defenders 1970–89

Bobby Moore

Moore was King among central defenders: the best example of a player who commanded respect not through raising his voice but because of who he was, the way he conducted himself and his peerless approach on the field. He was a big man on and off the pitch, big in stature and reputation and a giant of a player for club and country.

Moore was not the quickest but he was very intelligent. He knew just where to go to snuff out danger, his reading of the game for West Ham and England was vital. When he went to make his tackle, you knew who would be coming out the other side with the ball.

His marking of Pele in the England–Brazil game in the 1970 World Cup was one of the best displays of defending I have ever seen. There was mutual respect for each other which was demonstrated at the finish with that lovely embrace between two of the greatest names the game has known.

Phil Thompson and Mark Lawrenson

It is impossible to separate my two main Liverpool partners. Different types, contrasting styles, I enjoyed unbelievable success with the pair of them. If you combined the two into one you would have the perfect centre-back performer.

I have heard it said that Lawrenson and I were the best partnership that's ever been, but I think that's because our time together was in the eighties whereas my partnership with Thompson was further back.

My mum was quicker than Thommo but his speed was all in his head. He was better on the ball than Mark and when we were passing the ball between ourselves at the back, we could have kept it for three months. We conceded just 16 goals in 42 league games in 1979: a staggering achievement because, by his own admission, it was not one of Ray Clemence's better seasons.

We were never encouraged to play offside despite what the experts thought. We pushed up and held the line and if forwards ran into an offside position that was their fault. If the opposition were not caught twenty times in the first ten minutes, we would be disappointed.

Lawrenson was much quicker than Thompson. His recovery in the tackle was as good as I have seen. He was classy on the ball, though not as good as Thompson, and superior and more aggressive in the air.

Kevin Beattie

Those who played alongside him and those who played with him looked on Beattie as some kind of footballing Superman. A real *tour de force*, he had an imposing physique and was unstoppable in full stride.

He was quick for a big man and strong in the air. He was comfortable in possession and would slot easily into the full-back and midfield positions. What's more he regularly popped up with valuable goals from set plays. It was a tragedy that he had to finish early because there was obviously so much more to come, both for Ipswich and for England.

Roy McFarland and Colin Todd

McFarland was another footballing defender while Todd's strengths were as a tenacious tackler. Both were good players in their own right but at Derby they had a wonderful understanding and that is the secret of a successful flat back four.

In his early days, Todd looked as if he could have been an England regular for years to come. He suffered because of the excellence and the leadership qualities of Bobby Moore and later he faced severe competition from Phil Thompson. He was a dogged defender and with his speed it was difficult to get away from him. Todd always seemed to be there snapping at your heels.

McFarland was the complete all-round centre-half, very mobile and good on his feet. If the ball was anywhere near him in the air, you could guarantee he would win it, even though at 5ft 11ins he was not the tallest.

Rest of the World central defenders 1970–95

Franz Beckenbauer

The hallmark of greatness is the ability to create time and space and nobody has surpassed Beckenbauer in that respect. He was unflappable, so calm and composed he looked capable of going on for ever.

Beckenbauer was terrific as a midfield player but in the sweeper role he was the master. He epitomised the positive side of the position, mopping up in defence and then striding regally downfield to construct attack after attack with wonderful raking passes, often scoring himself. He wasn't the quickest but when a player reaches his level of performance, exceptional pace isn't even a consideration.

Daniel Passarella

A tough, uncompromising defender, Passarella was a superb tackler and for his height was brilliant in the air. Very much a left-sided player, he was good on the ball without being exceptional. However, his leadership qualities for Argentina were invaluable.

They were never better demonstrated than against the Dutch in the 1978 World Cup Final. After his side let slip a one-goal lead, Passarella went to work on them, demanding one last effort. Two goals in extra time sealed the Argentines' victory. In such ways Passarella more than compensated for the technical deficiencies in his play.

Franco Baresi

When I consider AC Milan's phenomenal success over recent seasons, I keep coming back to the defence and the one man who made it all possible – Baresi. At the back he calls every shot. I have never in club football seen any player who spends so much time organising his defenders. Baresi tackles well, has good mobility and is an excellent reader of the game. He can also distribute the ball with both feet.

His performance in the 1994 World Cup Final for Italy against Brazil was incredible considering he had only just returned from a 23-day absence following an injury which required an operation. It was such a shame for so fine a statesman of the game that he should fire over his attempt in the penalty sequence at the end of the game.

Gaetano Scirea

The outstanding component of the Italian defence during the 1982 World Cup finals in Spain, Scirea's calm, calculating approach held his team together in a crisis.

He had all the attributes required of a top-class defender: astute positional sense, strength in the tackle, excellence in the air. His performances in the semi-final against Poland and in the final against West Germany were of a high calibre.

Maxime Bossis

Bossis was a defensive organiser who could play as well. I've always thought him to be underrated. In the 1986 World Cup, France had a team determined to attack and prepared to take risks. Their midfield was composed almost entirely of creative players and it made it more difficult for the players behind.

However, Bossis was a source of strength and inspiration. He seemed able to cope even against the most dangerous attacks and when France were up against it, invariably he was the one sorting it out.

Ruud Krol

The Dutch side of 1974 were one of the best the world has seen and Krol was every bit as important to them as Johan Cruyff or Johan Neeskens. Krol's all-round game was magnificent – he had strength and pace, showed good footwork and in possession invariably chose the right options.

He could have played anywhere on the pitch, but the sweeper position, in a side who were the first exponents of total football, was perfect for him because he was so adept at coming out from defence to play.

It would have been fitting had Krol included a World Cup winners' medal in his collection, like those other renowned Dutchmen mentioned above. He was twice on the losing side and in the 1974 finals pushed Beckenbauer very close as the outstanding defender of the tournament.

British and Irish central defenders 1990–95

1 Gary Pallister
2 Tony Adams
3 Paul McGrath
4 Steve Bruce
5 Colin Hendry
6 Des Walker

British and Irish central defenders 1970–89

1 Bobby Moore
2 Phil Thompson and Mark Lawrenson
4 Kevin Beattie
5 Roy McFarland
6 Colin Todd

British and Irish central defenders 1970–95

1 Bobby Moore
2 Phil Thompson and Mark Lawrenson
4 Kevin Beattie
5 Roy McFarland
6 Paul McGrath

Rest of the World central defenders 1970–95

1 Franz Beckenbauer
2 Ruud Krol
3 Daniel Passarella
4 Gaetano Scirea
5 Franco Baresi
6 Maxime Bossis

Super Six

1 Franz Beckenbauer
2 Bobby Moore
3 Ruud Krol
4 Daniel Passarella
5 Gaetano Scirea
6 Franco Baresi

MANAGING THE RIGHT WAY

For many players, the logical next step when their career is over is to find a manager's job somewhere. It never appealed to me. After fourteen years at the top I had had enough, the stresses and strains had taken their toll and to step into a situation where the pressures are multiplied tenfold didn't strike me as a particularly good idea.

In my final season, 1989–90, we were being chased for the title by Aston Villa and towards the end I wasn't sleeping at all well. I stayed awake mulling over the next fixtures, working out all the likely results and permutations. The tension was getting to me.

At the back of my mind I was well aware that my career was coming to a close and this would probably be my last title to win. It's why I was so desperate to finish on a triumphant note. The playing was not a problem, even though by this stage I was coming up to my 35th birthday. It was just the thought that we were so close it would have been awful to have lost it.

Two months before I finally left the club, in February 1991, I had reached my decision to retire. There was no miracle cure to free my knees of pain. Liverpool suggested that nothing was said until the end of the season, which suited me fine. I busied myself doing a little coaching, seeing if I wanted to take a job in that area. I quite enjoyed it but the problem was my knee was so bad that I couldn't join in the training games. I knew it was going to be difficult standing on the sidelines unable to participate. I had never been a great spectator.

So that was the situation when, in the February, Kenny Dalglish quit as manager and I found myself 6–4 on with the bookies to take over. I went to the board and said it was unfair having such speculation when I had no desire to be the next man in charge. I didn't want to mislead the fans.

My first thought was that I was friendly with too many people in the dressing-room and it wouldn't have worked. The board suggested I bring my retirement announcement forward because, had it been left to the end of the season as planned, it might have looked like I was getting out because I hadn't got the job.

Of course, I couldn't leave without one last wind-up. After Kenny went, Liverpool had lost at Luton and were then knocked out of the FA Cup by Everton. I said to Ronnie Moran and Roy Evans that I was leaving the next day but, as the lads were a bit down, perhaps I should give them a lift by announcing I was to be the next boss.

We called the squad in for a meeting. 'You'll know why you're here,' I began, 'I'm to be the next manager. I've been in this dressing-room a long time and things will be different.' I said, 'I know where everybody drinks in Southport – that pub is out of bounds. I know where everybody drinks in the Wirrall – that pub is also out of bounds.' Then I said, 'We're going to video all the games and on the Sunday we'll come in, have a bit of lunch and run the film through. And, one last thing, nobody will have anything on in the afternoons because three times a week we'll be back for extra training.'

I asked if anyone had anything to say. There was silence, apart, that is, from Bruce Grobbelaar who muttered: 'We're all behind you, boss.' I walked out of the dressing-room and three young apprentices came running past me in the corridor. It shows how quickly word gets around because when I went into the players' lounge there they were on the telephone urging whoever was on the other end to get to a bookmaker. 'Put as much as you can on Alan Hansen to become the new Liverpool manager,' they demanded.

I realised then that things were getting out of control so I went back to the dressing-room. As I got closer I could hear the murmurings: 'Hansen this and Hansen that' and 'he's a . . .' I burst through the door. 'Only kidding, lads,' I said, 'I'm actually retiring.'

British and Irish managers
1990–95

Alex Ferguson

Ferguson left me out of Scotland's World Cup squad in 1986 and hurt my professional pride but there are no grudges from me and it would be churlish not to recognise his outstanding achievements over the last five years.

He has brought Manchester United back to where they belong so that now it's considered a disaster if they only finish second in the table.

Ferguson came very close to winning the double in two successive years, which would have been a unique achievement. He has bought players who were assets on the park and managed to show a profit when those players were sold on. He has also developed a youth structure that promises to make United the team to beat for the next five years as well. He is very protective of his players and his club and although that has brought him criticism at times it is undoubtedly a strength for a manager.

He is not afraid to gamble and took a risk with Eric Cantona at a time when Howard Wilkinson found that he could no longer work with him. He decided he could do without Paul Ince after a season during which the England midfielder had excelled; and he had faith in Paul Scholes's emergence which left Mark Hughes to find employment elsewhere.

Kevin Keegan

Not only has Keegan revived a sleeping giant, he has done it with style and an exciting, expansive game.

At Newcastle he's bought and sold plenty but that has to be the way to ensure success at the highest level. He was criticised for selling Andy Cole and went out to confront the fans massed at the gate to explain why he had agreed the deal. That showed real personality and style.

He reinvested the money in Les Ferdinand who has succeeded in improving the side. Ferdinand gives Newcastle so many more options. When they are defending they can launch the ball forward where his ability in the air, his pace, his strength, give them the chance of creating something from nothing.

Kevin likes to be close to his players and there will be plenty of laughter on the training pitch, though I'll wager his players know when it's time for the joking to stop and the serious stuff to begin.

George Graham

It always intrigued me how Graham managed to find so much success at Arsenal on a restricted wages policy. That is more the work of a magician than skilful management! It is sad the way his Highbury career ended because he had made Arsenal the most outstanding club side in the country. I also think it's unfair the way his teams were labelled dull and tedious to watch. If you go back over the championship-winning season of 1989, there were times when they went away from home and won by threes and fours.

The 'boring Arsenal' tag came about because they had a solid, mean defence but you don't win anything without one. Look at some of their results over the years – they went to Standard Liège in the Cup Winners' Cup in 1993 and scored seven away from home without reply. How many boring teams do that?

Kenny Dalglish

Dalglish's achievement in winning the championship for Blackburn is, in my view, unparalleled. Some people think that the money he's had to spend has given him an unfair advantage but that's missing the point. For one thing it is impossible to win the title without money: twenty years ago maybe, but not in this day and age. Also you could give anyone £50 million to spend and they wouldn't have the success that Kenny has found at Ewood Park.

For a start Alan Shearer would not have gone to Blackburn if Kenny hadn't been there. He would have signed for Manchester United or Liverpool. Then there are his other purchases, his value-for-money buys. Graeme Le Saux arrived for little more than a million – and became England's first choice left-back. Tim Sherwood cost peanuts from Norwich – and matured to lead the side to championship success. In addition Dalglish has also put a youth policy in place which will benefit the club for years to come.

It was a shrewd move to make Ray Harford his number two. An excellent coach, Harford's great value to Kenny in the early days was his Second Division experience. If Kenny had gone to Blackburn and said: 'I'm not abandoning my principles, I'll stick to the methods that brought Liverpool success,' he wouldn't have got into the Premier League, let alone won it.

I thought it unfair that Blackburn were criticised in their championship-winning season for their way of playing. It was said that they were not in Manchester United's class as a team who would entertain and excite us. Let's look at that more closely. Blackburn knocked the ball forward to Shearer, United knocked it forward to Mark Hughes. Both teams defended the 18-yard line and then hit opponents on the break; the only difference was that United broke quicker. In contrast to the likes of Keane, Ince, Kanchelskis and Giggs, Blackburn took a bit more time getting forward.

I believe that talk about entertainment is misguided. Ask the fans what they would prefer – success or entertainment. It would be success every time. The only managers I hear going on about the need to entertain are those at the bottom of the table.

Bobby Robson

For longevity and an ability to keep on producing winning teams, Robson has set imposing standards. His Ipswich sides were a constant threat to Liverpool at the end of the seventies and early eighties, he took England further in a World Cup competition than any other manager since Alf Ramsey and subsequently has gone on to win domestic championships in Holland with PSV Eindhoven and in Portugal with FC Porto.

It is a sensational record but I know it will always be a disappointment to him that he was unable to get his hands on our First Division title. His teams always had a reputation for playing progressive, attractive football, and considering his limited funds at Portman Road it was a miracle that he kept them so high for so long. It was significant that after he began his reign as England manager Ipswich began to slide and went out of the top flight.

With England I often felt Robson didn't enjoy the best of luck. In the 1988 European Championship in West Germany, he had possibly the strongest attacking foursome of the sides taking part, in Gary Lineker, Peter Beardsley, John Barnes and Chris Waddle. However, from the way Barnes and Beardsley performed for Liverpool against Wimbledon in the FA Cup Final, it was clear that they were spent physically and would be of little use to their country. They had played something like sixty matches in a high-tension season and were exhausted.

I can't remember one year at Liverpool when I wouldn't be counting down the days from April until the end of the season. I could not wait for it to finish. By that stage most players are so tired they long for a rest. It's a mental tiredness as much as physical. To expect these guys to play in World Cups and European Championships after a long, hard season, is tough because by then they are good only for lazing on the beach.

It was the same with Shearer in the 1995 Umbro Cup competition. He had won a championship medal, enjoyed a few celebrations and couldn't handle the thought of more football. He was shot, physically and emotionally. The only ones saying players should be able to play sixty games a season and then go off and play somewhere else in a major competition are those who have never had to do it.

However, in Italy in 1990 I thought Robson was lucky to take England to the semi-finals. They weren't that special a team; Belgium played them off the park and they were fortunate to get past Cameroon in the quarter-finals. Having said that, they would have won the final against Argentina had they beaten Germany in the semi-final penalty decider.

Jack Charlton

The Republic of Ireland teams have always had a terrific team-spirit and that reflects highly on Charlton. As a manager, he could be a hard, difficult man when he wanted to be, that much seems pretty obvious, but then show me a successful manager who wasn't. The Liverpool lads like Ronnie Whelan and Ray Houghton loved him and that's good enough for me. They appreciated that Jack treated them like adults. If they wanted a couple of pints of Guinness he would allow it – as long as they bought him one as well!

Much has been said about the methods Jack employed with Ireland, about his liking for a direct style from which midfield artists like Liam Brady are excluded. It's been said that if he had been in charge of England he would have played a different way, but how can you be so sure? I bet if he thought the strength of the team lay in playing that way, he would have done exactly the same.

A lot of nonsense is talked about tactics. In the debate over whether to use a one- or two-striker formation, all I would say is that the continentals have been using just the one man up front with the other tucked behind for about thirty years. It has happened in this country too. Look at the Liverpool teams – Rush was the lone striker with Dalglish playing just off him and slightly withdrawn, the same as when John Toshack was the target and Keegan played a shade deeper. Another example is Aston Villa's 1982 European Cup-winning side – Peter Withe was the target man with Gary Shaw dropping off.

Then there's the matter of the sweeper system. I have heard expert after expert and manager after manager say that the only way to win at world level is with a sweeper. So what happens in the 1994 World Cup? The two best teams in the competition, with the best defensive records, get to the final and they use a flat back four. In fact, nearly all the teams in America played with a flat back four, so where does that leave us?

The only conclusion is that it's players who are important, not systems. For me, the way for British sides to gain success on the wider stage is to integrate traditional British strengths – the three Ps, power, pace and passion – with higher technical ability. We have never been as good in that regard as the continentals. Even in 1966 there were superior technical sides to England.

The pace of the British game has got to be used to our advantage when we take on other nations. Our players can up the tempo and destroy the opposition. We should learn to recognise strengths and weaknesses. The managers I played under at Liverpool used to preach that we should play to our strengths and try to exploit the other side's weaknesses. And if you've a weakness yourself – and every team has – try to cover it.

British and Irish managers
1970–89

Bill Shankly

Any managerial analysis of this period has to start with the man whose legacy not just to a football club but to an entire city, can never accurately be measured. Shankly laid not only the foundations of Liverpool legend but virtually all the bricks and mortar as well.

They were a Second Division outfit going nowhere when, in 1959, Shankly steamed into Anfield. By sheer force of personality and a desire and commitment that recognised no obstacle, he built a sporting institution that not only rewarded him with trophy-winning success but paved the way for others to come along and add to his achievements. The passion for the club that impressed everyone who came in contact with him had the power of a tidal wave, it carried everyone along. His magnetism was irresistible, his enthusiasm overwhelming and enticing. The principles he laid down were such that even after he left, the flow of trophies to Anfield was maintained. Bob Paisley and Joe Fagan were great managers in their own right and Shanks's work helped them to achieve success. Everything was already in place.

The team-spirit Shanks fostered was a cornerstone for success for years to come. People who sneer at the value of team-spirit haven't been at a club where it has thrived. If you share that special feeling of comradeship and camaraderie you know you're ahead before you start. All the managers who followed Shankly have stressed the importance of an *esprit de corps*, of eating together, travelling together, doing everything as a group. They have continued it and encouraged it in every way possible.

Under Paisley we used to have a meeting on a Friday. It was really only an excuse to get together and have a laugh but it worked. When Kenny Dalglish took over, he would bring in the biscuits and we'd all sit around with mugs of tea and talk, not about the game the next day but about life in general.

It might sound trivial but the importance of being together on those occasions should not be understated. The next time we'd be together was the most important time of all – when we were preparing to get out on the pitch for business. Even if we were away training somewhere Kenny would maintain the ritual, ordering the biscuits and sorting out a place for us to have a natter.

Brian Clough

I could not have played under Clough and I think that goes for everyone I was with at Liverpool. It was just a phenomenal way of treating players, he had to be in total control. The players always appeared to have to be on their toes and watching their every step and that would have driven me mad. The great thing about Liverpool was that the set-up was so relaxed. Training was a pleasure and that is what I missed most when I packed it in.

However, no one can argue with the facts and figures. It is a rare feat to have won the championship with different clubs and Clough made it with Derby and then Nottingham Forest, having in each case first to guide them out of the Second Division. From there he took Forest to two European Cup wins – an incredible achievement when you consider the problems our best club sides are facing in Europe now. At the time Forest were Liverpool's jinx team. They beat us in the League Cup and in the European Cup but in terms of ability they weren't on the same planet.

Not that Forest didn't have some great players; Clough had a very regimented style of play that would ensure the best from his team. If they were around today, with all the television exposure, they would receive much more criticism because the four in Forest's midfield hardly ever moved from their chosen positions. They were a disciplined, rigid unit.

Kenny Dalglish

One February morning after training I was let in on a secret. 'They've asked me to take over as manager,' said Dalglish. 'Joe Fagan wants to step down at the end of the season.' I was the only Liverpool player to be in on the news. It was a shock but at the same time I was delighted for Kenny.

I don't think he could turn the offer down though I admit I was a little concerned about our relationship. He was a close pal, still is, and I was unsure how the friendship would continue when he was having to look at things from the other side of the fence. In the event he made the move from dressing-room to boot-room so smoothly you couldn't spot the join. It was amazing.

In his first three months he allowed two Anfield stalwarts, Phil Neal and Alan Kennedy, to go and thereby established his command straightaway. He didn't go to training at Melwood on the team bus as before. He went in his own car. In small ways he made sure there was a distance between himself and the players. In other ways it was the same old Kenny. He would join in training and we would still take the mickey out of his performance, just like before.

Considering his achievements, I don't think he's been given enough credit for the six years he spent as Liverpool manager. In the first couple of seasons he was still playing and that was especially difficult because rest and relaxation were important for his game. I have never seen a player prepare so well for matches and as a manager there are 101 other things to do as well.

The season before he took over, 1984–85, Liverpool had won nothing and at the end of it the club was left reeling by the horror of the Heysel Stadium disaster. It was not a good time to be beginning your first job in management yet his debut season saw us clinch the double with Kenny scoring the winner at Chelsea to lift the championship. Then a few days later there we were at Wembley, beating Everton in the first all-Merseyside FA Cup Final.

It was fairytale stuff, yet only two months before, I remember telling Kenny that we would win nothing. I thought at the time it was the worst Liverpool side I had played in. I believed the players had shot it and were no longer good enough. There was just one new face, Steve McMahon from Aston Villa, and I felt we should have bought others. Kenny's reply was that the spirit was good enough, it just needed a little luck to get us off on a winning run and he was proved correct.

His record over six years at Anfield was sensational. After the double in '86 we came close again in '88 when Wimbledon beat us at Wembley, and again in '89 when Arsenal pipped us for the title in that incredible Anfield finale. We were on course again in 1990 but somehow contrived to lose an FA Cup semi-final against Crystal Palace when we were on top.

Dalglish's best attribute is his hunger for success, his desire to win. It rubs off on others. His favourite phrase is: 'effort, attitude and commitment'. They were the words we heard in the dressing-room more than any others and they helped to concentrate minds.

There haven't been many players he sold who would have a bad word against him. When he signed players he would personally take them round to look at houses and areas. Not many managers could be bothered with that.

Jock Stein

Stein was one of the giant figures of his trade, a big man and a great manager. He was hard, very hard, but he wasn't stupid. His encouragement for his players was total and they appreciated that. Jock knew players wouldn't make mistakes on purpose and understood that coming down hard on them all the time would not lead to better performances. If things had to be said, they were said at the right time and then forgotten. The grouse would not be allowed to linger. Bob Paisley was the same.

Stein experienced repeated success when he was in charge of Celtic. When he took over the national side I got to know him better. It was a difficult job for him because of the Anglo–Scottish divide, the belief in some quarters that the national side should consist of Scottish players playing in Scotland. Our team-spirit was not as good as it could have been, certainly not as strong as that of the present side. Things have improved because players have started to move from England to Scotland in greater numbers than before while the movement of players generally around Europe has increased.

Bob Paisley

Paisley was a man of few words but they were always words worth hearing. What he had to say invariably went to the heart of the matter and I am still reminded today just what a shrewdie he was. He would preach about how the first two yards of pace at the highest level were in your head; about how experience was everything; about how teams that win the championship are still celebrating three months later and suffering for it (we saw that with Blackburn); that there wasn't a player born who did not have a weakness; that it was foolish to rubbish the opposition.

In addition he was the most ruthless manager I have come across. He had this image as a kind, avuncular figure but when it came to team selection all feelings and sentiment went out of the window. The only thought that preoccupied him was choosing the best possible team for Liverpool, regardless of reputation or past performance.

In 1981–82 I missed nine games, of which Liverpool won eight and drew one. On the Tuesday, I made my comeback in the reserves. On the Wednesday, a piece of glass fell on my thigh and required six stitches. That same night Liverpool went to Old Trafford and won 1–0. I trained on the Friday, still with stitches and still in some discomfort. Yet the next day, I was in the team and Terry McDermott was out.

Paisley was great at forgetting about last year, dismissing the fact that we had won something almost as soon as the day was over. Crucially, however, he would not forget *how* it was won. Complicated principles and philosophy were not for him – he kept it simple. And his record in the transfer market was second to none. He signed Dalglish, Souness, Rush, Lawrenson, Whelan, Kennedy, McDermott and Phil Neal. He also bought me although he had never seen me play!

Don Revie

There has been a lot of negative comment about Revie's famous Leeds sides of the sixties and seventies but winners will always attract criticism. People don't like them – unless they're a winner themselves. Revie's Leeds are talked about as a mean, physical side. I wouldn't say that Eddie Gray, for instance, fits that particular bill but the general point to be made is that there hasn't been a successful team yet who weren't able to stand up for themselves.

Look at the players Revie employed. Billy Bremner and Johnny Giles were the outstanding examples but they were all footballers with an extremely competitive edge. Sometimes they were near the knuckle with some of their methods but you can't deny that they made a lot of friends with the football they played.

The team appeared to have no weaknesses. Revie's secret was the team-spirit he fostered at the club. He took criticism for the carpet bowls and bingo games he introduced into the England set-up but I can't stress enough how important it is to get the players together. Whether it's carpet bowls or pool tournaments, it doesn't matter just as long as the players are together and enjoying what they're doing.

British and Irish managers 1990–95

1 Kenny Dalglish
2 Alex Ferguson
3 George Graham
4 Kevin Keegan
5 Bobby Robson
6 Jack Charlton

British and Irish managers 1970–89

1 Bill Shankly
2 Bob Paisley
3 Kenny Dalglish
4 Jock Stein
5 Brian Clough
6 Don Revie

Super Six

1 Bill Shankly
2 Bob Paisley
3 Kenny Dalglish
4 Jock Stein
5 Brian Clough
6 Don Revie

GOLDEN GOALS

An easy category this – not too many to choose from at all! It's a
certainty that with all the splendid goals scored between 1970–95
you could pick on six and quickly discover another sixty as good
or even better than your selection. Still here goes . . .

Goals: 1990–95

I could not leave out **Matt Le Tissier** in a current list of golden
goals; he seemed at one stage to have a monopoly on outrageous
strikes. In 1995 the Southampton playmaker deservedly won Goal
of the Season with his effort at Blackburn when he picked up the
ball not far over the halfway line, bamboozled two opponents
with outstanding control and ball manipulation before unleashing
a cunning lob which just cleared Tim Flowers and dropped
under the bar.

Some goals turn out to be even more important than they
seemed when they were scored. One that sticks in the mind is
Mark Hughes's volley in the 1994 FA Cup semi-final that earned
Manchester United a replay and served to deflate Oldham. At the
time United were struggling for form and looked dead and buried in
the game. They went on to win the replay and the FA Cup itself but
Hughes's cracker could also have ensured them the championship
prize that season. Who knows how United would have reacted to

going out one step from the final to a side who were on the way
to relegation?

Dalian Atkinson caught the eye with one of his early goals for
Aston Villa. It came at Wimbledon when he seized hold of the ball
inside his own half, set off on a mazy run and went clear of all
pursuers. The finish was dazzling, a subtle chip over Hans Segers
completing a wonderful example of intuitive skill.

Another excellent runner with the ball at his feet is **Steve
McManaman** who scored two identical goals to secure Liverpool
the 1995 Coca-Cola Cup at Bolton's expense. The best was the
first, as he cut in on an unstoppable run from the left touchline,
taking on and beating defenders before gliding his shot past
the keeper.

It's the World Cup goals that stay longest in the memory.
Roberto Baggio scored with a splendid effort in the 1990 finals
against Czechoslovakia, which he initiated from just inside his
own half. It had the lot, a neat exchange of passes and then a
deceptive run which ended with the Italian putting the defender
on his backside before finishing in some style.

Four years later in America the one that stood out for me
came against Bulgaria in the semi-final. Collecting the ball from
a throw-in, **Baggio** shrugged off two defenders as he came within
shooting range and dispatched another devilish shot, heavy and
with sufficient curl to take the ball into the corner of the net.

Goals: 1970–89

George Best made a habit of scoring goals that made you wonder
just how he managed to pull it off. They seemed beyond the reach
of ordinary players. A great example came at Old Trafford against
Sheffield United when he picked up the ball and set off on a
remarkable run which took him past three or four defenders to
the right-hand of the goal. It looked like he had taken the ball
too far but with wonderful balance and dexterity Best was able
to hook the ball home from a difficult angle.

Another stroke of genius was pulled by **Diego Maradona** in the

1986 World Cup quarter-final for Argentina against England. It came shortly after his 'Hand of God' effort and while that controversy was set to rumble on for a little while yet, his second goal left no room for doubt that he deserved to be the match-winner.

He was a good ten yards in his own half when he picked up possession, instantly drifting away from the two Peters, Beardsley and Reid. As he advanced over the halfway line he generated speed and power and it was impossible to halt him as he went past Terry Butcher and Terry Fenwick, drawing Peter Shilton off his line before rounding him in the perfect *coup de grâce*. It was then a simple task to slide the ball home; a magnificent triumph for skill under severe pressure.

In 1978 in his home country, **Mario Kempes** proved irresistible in front of the posts and was able to conjure up goals from the unlikeliest of situations. His pair in the final were priceless and a similar effort against Peru in the group games was equally valuable, helping Argentina reach – and pass – the four-goal target they needed to progress to the next stage. Having engineered a smart one–two just outside the area, Kempes showed remarkable poise and control to fasten onto the return before scything his way through the remnants of the back line, holding off two defenders before driving the ball low into the net.

It might seem strange, given his stupendous skills on the ground that kept defenders bemused and confused, to highlight a **Pele** header but for a small man he could be devastating in the air. From such a situation he opened the scoring in the 1970 final against Italy. He not only got up well to meet Rivelino's left-wing cross, he showed an incredible ability to hang in the air before finding the perfect placement with his header.

In the 1988 European Championship finals, **Marco Van Basten** finished off a highly impressive personal tournament with a crushing volley, cleanly struck and fiercely hit from an angle tight by the goal-line from where it looked impossible to score. It confirmed Holland's victory over Russia and the technique he revealed in that instant showed the powers he possessed.

Terry McDermott's spectacular goals were legendary. His exquisite lobbed efforts in vital cup encounters against Aberdeen and Everton could both have qualified here. However, for outstanding team-work, coordination and determination there is nothing to

better the one with which he rounded off our 7–0 drubbing of
Spurs at Anfield in September 1978. The move began with him
defending his own penalty box at a Spurs corner. As it developed,
he made up an immense amount of ground and arrived in the
opposing 18-yard box to supply the finishing header when the
left-wing cross came over.

ME AND MY BIG MOUTH

It's so easy to make a fool of yourself in this game, as I have found firstly as a player and now as a television 'expert'. Everyone has opinions and sometimes we rush to judge a player before it is really fair. He may be a youngster still trying to find his way or an expensive signing who has not had time to settle into his new surroundings. On occasion things are said which you later have cause to regret, but at the BBC they tell me it's all part of the fun!

Ian Rush

After Rush's first games for Liverpool I ventured the opinion that he would never make a player. I played alongside him in the reserves against Preston and on the opposite side that day was John Blackley who I knew from his time with Hibernian and Newcastle.

Blackley asked me afterwards what I thought of Rush because he hadn't been impressed. I said I believed Liverpool would sell him. He hadn't shown any of the speed or penalty-box instincts which he was about to become famous for and which would establish him as one of Liverpool's greatest-ever players.

Four years later, during which time Rush had scored about 250 goals for the club, I was having another drink with Blackley. He recalled our earlier conversation and joked, 'We're good judges, aren't we?'

Rushie knows what I thought of him at the time and we often laughed about it later. It's typical of him that he took it so well, and it was a real pleasure to watch him develop into such a formidable marksman.

Alan Ball

I said to Ball during a game against Southampton in 1981: 'What have you ever won in the game?' I was soon made to regret it.

He had clicked my heels a couple of times and we were having a bit of a spat. I lost my temper and said what I said. Of course, at that moment I was forgetting Ball was part of England's World Cup-winning team of 1966, one of only eleven players from these islands to have had the privilege of climbing the game's highest peak.

After my jibe, Ball turned round and said, 'Just the big one, son.' I heard him clear enough but at first I did not twig. So I asked Phil Thompson what he meant. 'I think he means the World Cup, Al,' replied Thommo, trying hard to hide his grin. Embarrassing or what!

Eric Cantona

When Cantona first played for Manchester United he was still a bit of an unknown quantity in English football. He hadn't played that many times for Leeds and I hadn't seen enough to be convinced he was going to emerge as the big personality.

In one of his first United appearances he was flicking the ball here and flicking it there. I don't really go for all that stuff and I made the comment that it's OK doing that in front of your own supporters when your are winning 4–0, the true test of a player comes away from home when you're 2–0 down.

Of course he passed that particular test some time ago. I was implying that Cantona may not have been a wholly committed, 90-minute man, that he turned it on only when he wanted to but the observation does not stand analysis beside his contribution for United over the last three seasons.

John Barnes

I wish I had never agreed to accept Barnesie's challange for the Liverpool FC handicap sprint at Aintree on Grand National Day. We had played in the morning and then gone to the races to enjoy ourselves with a few drinks. John and I were always winding each other up about who was the quickest and on this particular afternoon things got out of hand.

He challenged me to a 100 yards sprint up to the Melling Road and when he offered me a five-yard start and a £20 prize there was no holding me back. Off came the jackets as we persuaded one of the gatemen to stand by the rail and give us the off. It was just like the real thing. Our starter got to '2' and I was away and running, never to look back. I absolutely slaughtered Barnesie. He had played in the morning so would have stiffened up by then, but for my part I had not played for nine months and was hardly 100 per cent fit.

Looking back it was not the best of ideas. We had on our ordinary shoes but thankfully the going was not too bad although as I recall it wasn't good for Barnesie who tweaked a hamstring!

Everyone who had been in the hospitality marquee with us went out onto the balcony to cheer the two of us home. Terry McDermott saw it all because he was running a hamburger stall at the time and was just leaving the racecourse. He was waiting in a queue of traffic and said to his mate: 'Look at these two idiots coming up the track.' When he saw who it was he couldn't believe it.

Matt Le Tissier

I wish I had never said: 'Matt Le Tissier is a super de luxe luxury player.' I should have left it at 'super de luxe'. If you consistently score, and create, the number of goals that Matt does season after season, you can't be labelled a luxury performer.

Norwich

I wish I had never said that Norwich were not good enough to win the championship in the 1992–93 season. As it turned out I was absolutely right, but I know it caused a lot of resentment among their followers. The Canaries eventually finished third behind Manchester United and Aston Villa although I must admit there was a time late on when they were top and I was thinking it was going to be a bit too close for comfort.

I just didn't think they had enough good players to win it but they lasted the course extremely well. I took some stick about it but when I went to Carrow Road the following season for the Uefa Cup campaign, the supporters could not have been nicer to me.

Year after year they remain the same, the comments in the newspapers and in television interviews from those managers whose teams are at the top of the table. The same goes for those who are struggling near the bottom: it is as though they have a list of sayings that they can pull out according to the situation they are in.

⚽   ⚽   ⚽

Six things they say at the top

'Winning is everything' . . . said at the start of the season and after every victory.

'First is first and second is nowhere' . . . said when they're top with a good chance of finishing the season in first place.

'If we can't get first let's make sure we're second' . . . a change of tune, now it doesn't look as if they can get to first place.

'We've won nothing yet' . . . they're ten points clear with four games to go but the champagne remains on ice.

'Sometimes the points are more important than the performance' . . . they've played poorly but just scraped through.

'Never mind the crowd, just get it back to the keeper' . . . they're at home, 1–0 ahead, there's ten minutes left and they're holding onto the points but the crowd are getting restless because they're not playing like true champions-in-waiting. In these circumstances you just have to close your ears to what the fans are demanding.

Six things they say at the bottom

'Things can only get better' . . . they've just lost 6–0.

'There's no way we're abandoning our principles and philosophies' . . . they will stick to their way of playing, the so-called right way to play the game, even though it clearly doesn't suit them and will take them down.

'We'll be back on the training ground first thing Monday morning to put things right' . . . they'll keep working at it, no one can accuse them of slacking.

'We are not playing badly but we just need a break' . . . they have tried every other excuse, now their faith is pinned on lucky suits and black cats.

'We've got nine players out injured, you've got to expect us to struggle' . . . even though seven of the nine would not get in the team when fully fit.

'If you think there's pressure at the top, you should try it at this end of the table' . . . it gets lonely down here.

WING WIZARDS

There is no more exciting spectacle in football than wingers confronting defenders at speed, and leaving them trailing in their wake with a dip of the shoulder or a shimmy of the hips. They can bring spectators to their feet with a dynamic surge down the line but it should not be forgotten that wingers also have an important defensive role for their team.

Ninety-five per cent of wingers are hopeless at tackling so you don't want to put them in that situation. They've just got to drop back and use their intelligence to hold their position and become an obstacle to the other side. It's more common sense than anything else.

Many great wingers have added dash and style to the game – nearly all of them Scots I'm delighted to say! Peter Lorimer and Charlie Cooke, to name but two, were among those to miss out from my selection. So did Steve Coppell, a different sort of wide man from those mentioned below but a valued performer for Manchester United and a prime example of a winger willing to work.

There was a time when the man hugging the flanks, frequently frustrating but capable of great moments of flair, went out of fashion but the nineties have seen several outstanding young players emerge. As teams work harder to close opponents down in the midfield areas, so the value of someone who can offer width, dribbling skills and the ability to produce telling crosses, becomes greater.

British and Irish wingers 1990–95

Ryan Giggs

When he first played for Manchester United, Giggs was capti-
vating. Pacy and skilful, he had the knack of scoring eye-catching
goals. His career went backwards for a time which is a phase most
young players have to go through, particularly those who play in
the attacking positions, as teams work out how to neutralise their
strengths. He also picked up a few injuries but he has got over
those and the 1995–96 season has seen him back to his best.

If you were nit-picking you would have to say his awareness of
team-mates in the last third of the field is not as good as it could
be. His final ball, his ability to see players in better positions and
bring them into the action with the telling pass sometimes lets him
down. It's an attribute you cannot coach – you've either got it or
you haven't.

Darren Anderton

Anderton has always been a strong runner but now he looks strong
on the ball as well. He is much harder to knock off the ball than
in his early days and for a winger that can make the difference
between success and failure. You can't question the talent of any

of the players on this list or the positive way they set about the game. In this era of the super-athlete, however, you need more than that. You need the strength to be able to play. I don't mean you have to be a weightlifter but you can't afford to be knocked off the ball. Darren can pass it and cross it, he has good skills.

Chris Waddle

If there is one player you would not wish to face when he's coming at you full pelt with the ball at his feet, it's Waddle. He can drop one shoulder and go either way. If Chris had you back-pedalling you were in trouble and he had the advantage of having a sound right foot so he could fool you into thinking he was going to use his left before coming back onto his right to hit it.

Waddle has enjoyed acclaim over a very long period when you consider he made his debut for Newcastle in 1980, and he came close to being included on the list for the earlier period with Barnes. He was inspirational in 1993 in Sheffield Wednesday's progress to the FA and Coca-Cola Cup Finals and his free-kick in the FA Cup semi-final against Sheffield United was as good as you are going to see. That season he was deservedly honoured as the Football Writers' Association Footballer of the Year.

Like Barnes, Waddle struggled to make the same impact for England as he did for his clubs. He also found the standard of defending in the international game to be inhibiting. However, his awareness of team-mates is an object lesson for young players. He has spent the majority of his later seasons in midfield and hits wonderfully accurate passes with the outside and inside of his left boot.

Steve McManaman

I played with McManaman in Liverpool's reserves when he was lightweight but with an obvious talent coming through. I felt then that he could be anything he wanted to be and I am delighted that he has confirmed the potential.

As with Anderton, a big improvement in McManaman's game over the last 18 months has been on the physical side. He is a lot stronger, a great deal more resilient now and cuts a splendid sight when running at speed with the ball. In fact he is as fast with the ball as he is without it and that is a rare gift. Steve is capable of scoring outstanding goals, though like Giggs he has to improve his vision and his appreciation of others.

Dennis Wise

Wise is a different proposition from the others in this section because he is not one you will see hurtling past two or three down the line. Terry Venables has called him another Alan Ball and I can see the similarities between the two of them.

I believe the Chelsea skipper has more talent than he is given credit for. He's talked about as a niggardly so-and-so but his competitiveness is a big plus for Glenn Hoddle's team. His use of the ball is first-class, he looks around for his team-mates and he knows exactly where he is going to put the ball.

Gordon Strachan

Just as Leeds must at times have regretted allowing Eric Cantona to leave, so there must also have been consternation at Old Trafford when Manchester United permitted Strachan to make the reverse journey and then saw him inspire Howard Wilkinson's class of '92 to the championship, beating his former club by four points.

Sometimes a player needs a change of scenery to inspire something extra. That was the case when Strachan went to Elland Road – he found a new lease of life. He has been a marvellous ambassador for his sport and a consistent performer through the years. He had an engine that lasted all day but that doesn't make him a great player. An engine but not much talent makes an all right kind of player but Gordon had outstanding ability as well.

He could hit the ball long or short, he knew where to go and when to go there, and he always seemed to find space for himself and his colleagues.

When Leeds signed David Rocastle as his replacement, Strachan's performances were so good that the former Arsenal man couldn't get a game and was eventually sold on. Strachan had speed and the tricks to go with it. He has never lacked heart and determination and his will to win is obvious. Any team-mates who have fallen from the high standards he sets himself and others are soon made aware of it!

British and Irish wingers 1970–89

George Best

Who else can start this section? Simply, George was the Best, the legend has been well documented. I never had the privilege of playing against him and I thank my lucky stars for that – just watching the television clips was enough to fill you with foreboding.

Sometimes you hear the older generation praising yesterday's stars and criticising the present day players and it's wise to retain some scepticism. Things always look more rosy with the passing of time but in George's case you know it is impossible to overstate his impact for Manchester United and Northern Ireland.

He was blessed with all the skills but also the physical strength and courage to go with it and that was equally as important. You don't earn so high a status in the world game without having that dimension to your play. Look at Pele, Maradona, Johan Cruyff and Best – along with massive talent they all possessed heart and strength. No matter how often they were kicked, and these guys would be kicked a lot more than most, they would never be afraid to come back for more.

Eddie Gray

Gray scored goals that stayed a long while in the memory, like the one against Burnley when he beat about 37 men and a dog in a slalom ride down the left flank. He also produced memorable individual displays for Leeds United such as in the 1970 FA Cup Final against Chelsea. The man had special ability.

Gray sparked things off with his wonderful left foot. He could ghost past people as if they weren't there. It did not matter if there were three or four defenders lined up to block his path, he would always find a way to get past.

At Wembley in 1970 he led the Chelsea full-back, David Webb, a merry dance, turning first this way and then that in a spellbinding exhibition of trickery. For the replay, Chelsea switched Webb and Ron Harris and although Gray remained full of menace it was the Londoners who had the last laugh as Webb grabbed the extra-time winner.

John Robertson

Robertson would never conform to the image of how a professional footballer should look, act and live his life, but he could really play. He was a little on the plump side and if I was going to race him over 50 yards I would be confident of giving him a start of ten and still leaving him for dead. But with the ball at his feet you couldn't get near him – he was another of those whose speed was in his head.

John had a neat side-step which enabled him to go inside or out and with two good feet you could never tell which way he wanted to go. That's tough for defenders because it's impossible to force him one way. With a little shuffle he could switch to the other side and clip the ball in with left or right foot.

Robertson was an integral part of Nottingham Forest's success in the seventies and eighties. The cross which laid on the winning goal for Trevor Francis in the 1979 European Cup Final against Malmo, sat up and begged to be put away. It had 'goal' written all over it. Possibly not the most disciplined footballer there has ever been but he could produce when it mattered and that's what counts. Brilliant at making space for himself.

John Barnes

There is no doubt that Barnes was one of the best I ever played with at Liverpool. I would put him in the top four along with Kenny Dalglish, Graeme Souness and Ian Rush. Barnesie's contribution to the team, both individually and collectively, was outstanding.

For my first ten years at Anfield, when I picked up possession there was one target I always sought out: Kenny Dalglish. In the last four years it was to Barnes that I would look every time. If you were under pressure, Barnesie was the outlet – he was that strong and had so much pace he could retain possession, give you some respite and get you back in the game.

He could be relied on to produce something extra whether it was to go past three or four players or supply the instant, masterful cross. His technical skills were of the highest order.

John's England form has been a mystery to most people and I agree that he never reproduced for his country the ability he showed week-in, week-out for his club. It's easy to forget how much more difficult it is at international level.

At Liverpool he could beat three men to score but how many times do you see that happen at the very highest level and I include all the great players in that. It just doesn't happen but Barnes is still expected to pull on an England shirt and beat half a dozen. He produced that outrageous goal against Brazil early in his international career and it became a burden – after that it was expected of him every time he took to the field.

I'm the first to admit that he was not as sensational for England as he was for Liverpool but I've come away from Wembley after international games, thinking he's not done bad. If not Barnes then who else could have come in and generated the fantasy and flair for England? Chris Waddle, maybe, but the general consensus is that he, too, never found his best form in his country's colours.

Even though Liverpool had good sides between 1987 and '90 and a great team in '88 when we went twenty-nine games undefeated, we would miss John when he was not playing. We wouldn't automatically struggle but it would be apparent that a very important cog was missing. As good as Dalglish and Souness were, if they weren't available they would not be so badly missed because they were surrounded by tremendous players in every position.

Jimmy Johnstone

You would have to kick Johnstone ten feet in the air if you wanted to stop him. Like Maradona, the little Celtic winger had great balance and would resist all attempts to dump him on the floor. Even in tight situations he was so adept at nipping in and out, evading all attempts to nick the ball from him. With a drop of his shoulder and a swerve of his hips, away he would go.

Johnstone proved to be a vital performer for Celtic on the big occasion, as Leeds found to their cost in the 1970 European Cup semi-final when he tore them apart. He was blessed with superb dribbling skills and rapid acceleration. He also packed a powerful right-footed shot.

Steve Heighway

We used to have a training routine at Liverpool which set two boards 40 yards apart. The forward would play the ball off one of the boards and set off on a run. A defender would be selected to go and meet him and try to take the ball from him. The idea for the attacker was to go round his opponent and strike the ball against the other board.

As a defender the player you prayed to avoid was Heighway because you could forget any idea of being able to stop him. He was as quick as I've ever seen over the first five or six yards and with his ability to con you one way and drift past you down the other, he was a handful. A supreme example of the advantage a player has with two good feet.

Rest of the World wingers 1970–95

Jairzinho

Jairzinho was a flying winger who not only went past defenders easily but also delivered a regular number of goals. In 1970 he became the first player to score in every round of the World Cup and his pace gave the Brazilians an important threat down both flanks.

Jairzinho had the ability to get behind defenders and then to make his advantage count. He had the composure to place the ball in the corner or chip the goalkeeper. When he decided to cross the ball his deliveries from the right touchline were always of a high quality.

Rivelino

Another from the Brazilian team of 1970, Rivelino operated on the opposite side of the pitch to Jairzinho and was a revelation with a repertoire of tricks that was enthralling to watch.

His left foot was made in heaven and he could use it to impart pace or swerve to the ball. Shooting on sight, he gave goalkeepers very little chance to make the save; and when taking free-kicks he was likely to render the defensive wall a waste of time. He could put so much curl on the ball that he could make it evade the last man in the wall and squeeze into the net.

Paulo Futre

Portugal's youngest international, Futre showed glimpses of his skill in the 1986 World Cup but he tended to be under-used in that competition and for a long time it was a commentary on his whole career. You knew there were great things that this wide man was capable of, but it seemed to take a long time for the message to hit home.

A wonderfully gifted talent, his run through the Bayern Munich defence which deserved to end with a goal was the highlight of Porto's European Cup victory over the West German side in 1987.

Eder

Eder could be inconsistent but on his day he was a winger who would tear the most orderly of defences to pieces. The Brazilian was the master of the dead ball, as Scotland found to their cost in the 1982 World Cup. He could swing the ball around the defensive wall with great success but, on this occasion, he showed an alert brain and executed a superb lob beyond Alan Rough for Brazil's third goal in their 4–1 victory over us.

Pierre Littbarski

Wonderfully elusive and daring, the diminutive German winger was around for three World Cups, sharing in the success of 1990 and the defeats in the finals of '82 and '86. That alone makes Littbarski worthy of mention.

Like Jimmy Johnstone, his size helped him to escape from

defenders, one touch either side of his marker and he was away. He kept battling away, a typical German in that respect, and weighed in with his share of goals. Mostly though his contribution came as a provider for others.

Brian Laudrup

Laudrup has everything you could wish for in a winger: the ability to go past players on either side, pace and skill, and a good awareness of those around him. For me, what stands out about the Rangers player is that while he scores a lot of goals himself, put him in a 2 v 1 situation and he will pass the ball to his team-mate. He is very unselfish and always works for the benefit of the team rather than personal glory.

His pace is an asset, of course, but where the Danish international scores over others is in his ability to stay on his feet. His balance is such that he can take a severe buffeting and still retain control of the ball.

British and Irish wingers 1990–95

1 Chris Waddle
2 Gordon Strachan
3 Steve McManaman
4 Ryan Giggs
5 Darren Anderton
6 Dennis Wise

British and Irish wingers 1970–89

1 George Best
2 Jimmy Johnstone
3 John Barnes
4 Eddie Gray
5 Steve Heighway
6 John Robertson

British and Irish wingers 1970–95

1 George Best
2 Jimmy Johnstone
3 John Barnes
4 Eddie Gray
5 Steve Heighway
6 John Robertson

Rest of the World wingers 1970–95

1 Jairzinho
2 Rivelino
3 Eder
4 Pierre Littbarski
5 Paulo Futre
6 Brian Laudrup

Super Six 1970–95

1 George Best
2 Jairzinho
3 Rivelino
4 Jimmy Johnstone
5 Eder
6 Pierre Littbarski

MATCHES MADE IN HEAVEN – AND THOSE NOT

Memorable matches 1990–95

1: Liverpool 3 Manchester United 3 – January 1994

Only very occasionally can a fixture be said to contain every-thing a spectator could want. This league game at Anfield fitted the bill perfectly – for sheer theatre, passion, courage, eye-catching goals and a sensational plot, it was the finest I have ever witnessed.

When United went 2–0 in front early on, around thirty Liverpool fans around me got up and walked out. At 3–0 twice that number decided to leave, vowing never to return. Yet there was still a long way to go and you can imagine their feelings later when they realised they had missed the glorious fightback. The final scoreline could easily have been 6–6.

With United coasting you would have thought that, with their defence and goalkeeper, there was no possible way back for Liverpool. In that situation the secret is to score quickly. Nigel Clough began their reply, and added another soon after, but in between United could have added three more themselves. After Neil Ruddock's second-half equaliser, Liverpool looked capable of snatching a winner.

A point at the home of their closest rivals was not disastrous for United, but considering the advantage they had created
for themselves they would have gone away with mixed emotions. Liverpool fans, on the other hand, were saluting a moral
victory.

2: West Ham 1 Manchester United 1 – May 1995

I can't remember spending so much of a game on the edge of
my seat. How United didn't score a second at Upton Park that
dramatic Sunday afternoon to claim the championship, I'll never
know. They will look at the video again and again and think 'we
must score here'. It was Custer's Last Stand and the Alamo all
rolled into one.

Andy Cole had chances galore, but each time Ludek Miklosko
was down to foil him. On one occasion the goalkeeper appeared
to be on the floor already, anticipating the low shot. A touch more
composure and Cole would have ensured the championship stayed
at Old Trafford. What made it so exciting was that at the same time
Blackburn were completing their programme at Liverpool knowing
that victory would make them champions. A draw would suffice if
United failed to win.

Blackburn went ahead, through Alan Shearer, naturally, and
when Michael Hughes scored for West Ham the fat lady was
preparing to sing and to signal the end of United's challenge for a
third successive crown. They had started the game without Mark
Hughes and it looked as if Alex Ferguson was going to pay the
price for a failed gamble.

With Hughes restored for the second half, United quickly
equalised. Their fans willed them forward for another which
became more imperative as news came through that Liverpool
had drawn level. One more United goal would have been enough
had the Anfield score stayed the same. In fact Liverpool snatched
a last-minute winner, but with United failing to turn their siege
into something substantial for a second time, Jamie Redknapp's
swerving free-kick proved irrelevant to the outcome. Blackburn
were champions for the first time in eighty-one years.

3: Everton 4 Liverpool 4 – February 1991

I missed this FA Cup fourth round replay through injury and was I glad I did. Liverpool were so bad defensively in the Goodison game, which turned out to be Kenny Dalglish's last before he quit, that I would not have wanted to be tarred with that brush. But what a spectacle! The first game had ended 0–0 and gave no hint of what was in store for the replay which has been called the finest cup-tie since the war.

Peter Beardsley scored a great first goal with his right foot after half an hour and Liverpool looked set to go through. We were moving forward sweetly but at the back it was a different story. Every time Liverpool scored they allowed Everton back in for an equaliser.

Beardsley hit a second late on after Graeme Sharp had equalised. Sharp quickly cancelled it out again. Ian Rush seemed to have put the tie beyond doubt but, with almost the final kick of normal time, the Everton substitute Tony Cottee sent it into extra time.

The pattern remained unchanged as the tension inside Goodison became almost unbearable. John Barnes chipped in a spectacular effort to point Liverpool to victory again but right at the end Cottee popped up a second time with another late Everton saver. It was so unlike Liverpool to concede that many goals and at crucial periods of the game. Everton won the replay by which time Kenny had left the club.

4: England 1 West Germany 1 (WG won 4–3 on penalties) – July 1990

I'm sure I'm not the only one who thought England were a touch lucky to make it into the World Cup semi-finals in Italy. They struggled to overcome Belgium who struck the woodwork twice and generally were the better team, and in the quarter-finals looked for a time to be giving second best to Cameroon.

However, against Germany fortune seemed to desert Bobby Robson's side. They fell behind to an Andreas Brehme shot that

took a wicked deflection off Paul Parker before looping over
Peter Shilton, had a couple of near misses and equalised through
Gary Lineker with ten minutes remaining to send the game into
extra time.

The excitement continued unabated. Chris Waddle struck a post,
so did the Germans. Paul Gascoigne's tears added to the drama
as the game inched towards the inevitable penalty shoot-out. The
score was three penalties apiece when Stuart Pearce's attempt
was saved and Waddle sent his into orbit. England went out
but I believe if they had won they'd have gone on to lift
the trophy.

5: Manchester United 2 Sheffield Wednesday 1 – April 1993

This was the game that clinched Manchester United's first championship for twenty-six years. Aston Villa's home defeat to Oldham
three weeks later was to confirm the feat beyond all doubt, but
if they had lost this Old Trafford fixture the chances are United
would never have recovered to push themselves over the finishing
line in first place.

Closing on the 90-minute mark, it looked as if they were
going to miss out again, just as they had the previous year to
Leeds. Wednesday were 1–0 ahead as the game was coming to
an end. There were only a couple of minutes left when Steve
Bruce ventured forward for a corner and scored. Deep into
injury time Bruce repeated the trick and United snatched all
three points.

Emotion and relief spilled out all around Old Trafford. Alex
Ferguson and Brian Kidd danced and hugged on the pitch following
each of Bruce's headers, going from despair to outright delight in a
matter of minutes.

With Villa held at home by Coventry, their victory against
the odds put United back on top by one point and provided
the impetus for them to go on and banish the memory of
twenty-six fallow championship years. They never looked back,
winning their final five games to end with a winning margin of
ten points.

6: Italy 2 Nigeria 1 – July 1994

Italy had not enjoyed a sparkling start to the World Cup. Beaten by the Republic of Ireland in their opening group game, they struggled to knock over Norway after their goalkeeper, Gianluca Pagliuca, was sent off. This second-round confrontation with Nigeria, the most exciting, uninhibited side in the tournament, was indicative of how their spirit and resolve grew out of the disappointment of poor team and individual displays early on.

Drawing their final group fixture with Mexico meant Italy scraped into the third qualifying spot as all four teams finished on four points. Meanwhile, Daniel Amokachi's last-minute goal against Greece put Nigeria on top of Group D and ensured they would meet Italy in Boston.

The fixture once again showed the two sides of the Italians. Nigeria, guaranteed the support of every neutral for the flair and enterprise they had brought to the tournament, went in front through Amunike midway through the first half as the Italians struggled to make an impression. Mentally they were preparing for the flight home when, with three minutes to go, Roberto Baggio equalised. It was the touch of a master for it looked a simple goal as he guided home a cross from the right, but the accuracy and weight he applied to the shot was sheer class.

Having a treasured victory snatched from them so cruelly, Nigeria were unable to recover and rarely threatened in extra time which saw Baggio claim the winner from the penalty spot.

Memorable matches 1970–89

1: Brazil 4 Italy 1 – July 1970

The 1970 Brazilians were the best side I have ever seen. For this World Cup Final, Italy were racked with caution, understandable in many respects given Brazil's decimation of the opposition in earlier rounds, and that invited the South Americans to come at them. The outcome was inevitable; Brazil, inventive and supremely confident, played quite beautifully.

Inevitably Pele was at the fulcrum of all their best work, scoring after 18 minutes with a prodigious header from Rivelino's corner. Italy were gifted an equaliser through a sloppy defensive mistake but it could not encourage them into a more adventurous approach and Brazil quickly regained the initiative.

Gerson hit a tremendous left-footed drive, Jairzinho surged into the penalty area to make it 3–1 but the best was saved to last. Jairzinho fed Pele who superbly carried the ball on for the advancing Carlos Alberto to drive home the fourth.

2: France 3 West Germany 3 (WG won 5–4 on penalties) – July 1982

This was the first time a penalty sequence had been employed to decide a tie in the World Cup finals but aside from that it was a highly dramatic affair. Unfortunately it is also remembered for the sickening challenge by the German goalkeeper Harald Schumacher which left the French substitute Patrick Battison unconscious and so badly hurt that there were fears he would die.

The moment proved to be a turning point for the Germans. The score was tied at 1–1 and Battison had looked certain to score as he raced through the middle of the German defence. Schumacher was allowed to remain on the field – referees today would surely have sent him off for dangerous play – and was able to play his part in Germany's shoot-out victory.

The reshuffle naturally came at the cost of French momentum and only two splendid saves kept them afloat. In extra time Germany sent on Karl-Heinz Rummenigge yet it was the French who took command and established a 3–1 lead. However, Germany are never beaten until the final whistle is blown. Rummenigge brought them back in touch and the centre-forward Klaus Fischer equalised. The Germans emerged 5–4 winners in the penalty shoot-out with the villain Schumacher pulling off two vital saves.

3: England 2 West Germany 3 – July 1970

England were reckoned to have the best organised defence in the world at the time and yet, incredibly, in this World Cup quarter-final they conceded three goals to lose the game after holding a 2–0 lead with only 22 minutes to play.

Germany played a crucial hand with the introduction of their substitute, the winger Grabowski, to run at a tiring defence and he gave his side new heart. Franz Beckenbauer equalised against the unfortunate Peter Bonetti, who answered an emergency call when Gordon Banks fell sick on the day of the game, and the veteran, Uwe Seeler, took the tie into extra time.

The initiative was clearly now with the Germans and it was left to the prolific Gerd Muller to slam the final nail in England's coffin. A wonderful match.

4: Arsenal 3 Manchester United 2 – May 1979

The following year Arsenal beat Liverpool in a marathon semi-final that went to four games and their resilient, never-say-die qualities had already been signposted in this FA Cup Final twelve months before. For 86 minutes the Wembley showpiece had not been particularly memorable. When Frank Stapleton scored Arsenal's second just before the break they looked home and dry.

United seemed dispirited but somehow they roused their tired limbs to produce an incredible finale, the like of which Wembley had not seen since 1953 and Stanley Matthews' finest hour. With four minutes remaining Arsenal still led by two goals. Their players admitted afterwards that in their thoughts they were already halfway up the steps to the royal box. But within 120 seconds they were brought rudely back to the present as United scored twice in rapid succession.

Gordon McQueen swept the ball home following a Joe Jordan cross and then immediately Sammy McIlroy went jinking into the Arsenal area before squeezing his shot past Pat Jennings. It was heady stuff which had the Gunners rocking but the last word belonged to them as Liam Brady, who had already laid on Arsenal's first two goals, created one more piece of magic. He played the ball wide to Graham Rix whose cross sailed beyond Gary Bailey's reach for Alan Sunderland to turn in.

5: Leeds 7 Southampton 0 – March 1972

A slaughter for the Saints in this league game; for Leeds virtually the perfect cocktail of skill, team understanding, fluency and ruthless arrogance. Towards the end it became an embarrassment as Don Revie's all-conquering side toyed with their victims, in one movement stringing together twenty-five passes without the opposition touching the ball. Each pass was greeted with a triumphant cheer from the 34,000 crowd as Southampton struggled to get a touch of the ball.

It was one of those rare occasions when all the flicks and all the party pieces came off. Billy Bremner and Johnny Giles thoroughly enjoyed themselves that day – tough professionals the pair of them, they relished piling on the misery.

6: Argentina 3 Holland 1 – June 1978

The World Cup Final in Buenos Aires was a thrilling, tense affair that required extra time to produce a winner. Just as four years before, the Dutch had been probably the best side in the earlier rounds but were below their best for the showpiece game against the host nation.

There was a physical edge to the final and early fouls set the tone for the event. Mario Kempes, the heartbeat of the Argentines with a phenomenal scoring touch, shot them ahead in the first half with a sweep of his devastating left boot after crashing through the defensive lines.

Fillol then kept the Dutch at bay with vital saves as Holland came more into it. With eight minutes left substitute Dirk Nanninga brought Holland level and Rob Rensenbrink struck the left-hand post with an opportunity that could have averted the need for the extra 30 minutes.

Argentina found a second wind in extra time as Kempes came on strong again. He received a pass, forced his way through a couple of challenges, somehow managing to retain his balance, and prodded the ball home. Then he created the opening for Daniel Bertoni to make it 3–1.

My most memorable Liverpool games

1: Liverpool 3 Arsenal 1 – August 1979

This was the finest performance by a Liverpool team in my time at the club. It was the Charity Shield, the traditional curtain-raiser to the season, an occasion when some teams don't bother as much as they would for a competitive game. Arsenal gave it their all – and still we murdered them, Terry McDermott (twice) and Kenny Dalglish helping us stroll to victory.

We passed the ball well, our movement off the ball was excellent, the combinations worked sublimely, everyone stood out. It was a superbly organised team performance and gave full warning of our intentions for the coming campaign. It was wonderful to play in and it must have been wonderful to watch as well.

It was even more special because at the start of any season with Liverpool you were playing for fitness. Training was organised so that you would not be fully fit in August and September. Come the crucial games in March and April, however, and we would be bombing while other sides were starting to flag.

After this particular fixture we began the season with only seven points from the first seven games. The old 'end of an era' stuff was churned out once more but we silenced the doom-merchants by embarking on a sixteen-match unbeaten run. After that we never looked back and at the finish had a two-point advantage over Manchester United.

2: Bayern Munich 1 Liverpool 1 – April 1981

We had drawn the Anfield leg of the European Cup semi-final 0–0 and Paul Breitner, one of the Bayern and German greats, savaged us in a television interview, claiming our technical skills were rubbish. That was bad enough but on the day of the return leg leaflets were placed on every seat in the stadium, showing the German supporters the way to Paris for the final! It was such an arrogant thing to do, but it worked to our advantage.

Coupled with what Breitner had said two weeks before, we were now really fired up! But it was a tall order to exact revenge for the double insult. We had a depleted side; Colin Irwin and Richard Money came in from the reserves and after seven minutes we lost Kenny Dalglish with an injury. Howard Gayle came on so we had three players involved who were not first-team regulars. It got worse – Gayle became involved in a fracas, was booked and had to be substituted to save him from a sending-off. Then, with 15 minutes left, David Johnson pulled a hamstring. He had to stay on – both our subs had been used.

It was at that moment that Bob Paisley came into his own. He knew we had no option but to try to win the game in 90 minutes, we could not last out in extra time with ten men and a passenger, so Ray Kennedy was switched into the middle. He scored what turned out to be a crucial away goal and although Bayern equalised with a minute to go we were through.

Our celebrations knew no bounds, we were so delighted to turn the tables. Six or seven of the lads pounded their fists on the Gemans' door. The noise in our dressing-room was incredible. We sang 'Gay Paree' at the top of our voices for about twenty minutes. Sweet revenge indeed.

3: Liverpool 3 Everton 1 – May 1986

This was extra special because it was my first FA Cup Final as well as the first all Merseyside FA Cup Final. It also clinched the double in my first season as captain.

There is no game quite like the Wembley showpiece at the end of the season. The pressure beforehand is unique, the build-up goes on for six or seven days and it becomes quite nerve-wracking. On this occasion, because of the interest in Liverpool in the clash between its two senior clubs, the tension was greater than ever.

We trailed to a Gary Lineker goal and until we scored could not have complained if Everton had been in front by three. Somehow we managed to grind our way back in, helped by an inspired Bruce Grobbelaar save when he pushed Graeme Sharp's header over the bar. We had just drawn level through Ian Rush and attacked with renewed confidence.

Craig Johnston put us 2–1 in front and then Ian Rush killed off hopes of an Everton comeback by hammering Ronnie Whelan's chipped pass across Bobby Mimms and into the far corner of the net. It was a contented captain who climbed Wembley's famous thirty-nine steps to collect the trophy.

4: Liverpool 5 Nottingham Forest 0 – April 1988

Some have described this as the best-ever Liverpool display but for me it does not rate with the Charity Shield victory over Arsenal because the opposition were not so good. We had beaten Forest in the FA Cup semi-final at Hillsborough the previous Saturday. For this league game they had one or two injuries, Des Walker came off after 15 minutes and thereafter they disintegrated.

Some of our football was exceptional. Peter Beardsley was at his devastating best. A couple of times he sent their defenders the wrong way with those mesmerising feints of his. If you watched the game again today, you would be baffled why we did not score eight, nine or ten, we were that superior. But to me it doesn't compare with the Arsenal game because on the day, Forest were a team waiting to be beaten.

We should really have had an adverse reaction to winning the semi-final because it seemed we had visited every boozer between Sheffield and Liverpool on the way home and on the Sunday eight of us went down to London for the annual Professional Footballers Association awards dinner. We trained on the Monday afternoon and you would have thought we would be struggling. As it turned out it was Forest who suffered the reaction.

5: Everton 0 Liverpool 5 – November 1982

Any Merseyside derby is a special occasion because of the rivalry and tension between the two clubs. Yet it never gets to that hysterical state where fans want to punch each other. There are families where the father and grandad support Liverpool and the sons follow Everton. The fans relish the conflict and the baiting that goes with it but, for the players, when the game starts it is a case, in a footballing sense, of kill or be killed.

One of my first Liverpool appearances was in a Merseyside derby. I have never experienced noise like it – not before nor since. It was one of those occasions when you really could not hear yourself think. I went into a pub in Anfield after the game and fans of both teams were mixing together there. I was still learning about the situation between the clubs and I assumed after a few drinks it would all go off, but they were still there much later, still discussing the game, high-spirited but good friends.

This particular league fixture was special because apart from the magnitude of the victory it ranks as one of my best-ever Liverpool performances. Ian Rush was absolutely lethal that day, scoring four times, two of which I laid on for him, but the all-round team display was excellent.

6: Liverpool 9 Crystal Palace 0 – September 1989

To score nine times against a team from the same division has to be a particularly special feat. Yet I remember coming off the pitch thinking Ian Wright and Mark Bright had played well and had posed us a few problems, which in a contest we had won 9–0 seems strange.

The goals flew in from all angles. It was just one of those nights. Even when the scoreline reached three and four and there was still a long way to go, we didn't visualise it reaching nine. Everyone seemed to get on the scoresheet except me. In fact, I don't think I got past the halfway line.

My worst Liverpool defeats

1: Liverpool 0 Arsenal 2 – May 1989

One of football's cardinal sins is to become distracted by what is at stake or what the opposition have to do to get what they want from the game. On this particular May evening, it was only natural that at the back of our minds was the knowledge that Arsenal had to beat us by two goals to take the trophy away from Anfield.

In all my years with Liverpool, and we are talking no less than 621 games, I can't remember losing at home by more than one goal. Yet on a scarcely believable night of decisive championship football, as both sides approached the season's final game still in a position to win and deny their closest rivals the prize, our own fortress was to fall apart. Even when Alan Smith scored in the first half to give Arsenal the lead, it didn't start any alarm bells. We still didn't realistically believe we would lose it and I don't think Arsenal really thought they would be taking the title back to north London either. With a minute remaining and our overall advantage intact, a time when it would have been the cruellest of cruelties to toss it all away, I don't recall there being any panic. We seemed nicely in control.

Then, well we all know what happened next. Michael Thomas broke away, seized on a pass from Smith, held his nerve and Arsenal won 2–0. The title was theirs in the most incredible fashion possible and we lost out. Yes, there were a lot of tired Liverpool legs that night but we can't honestly use it as an excuse. We had played in the FA Cup Final against Everton the previous Saturday, then faced West Ham on the Tuesday and because of Hillsborough had been forced to play a lot of games in a short space of time. We were drained emotionally rather than physically.

It goes without saying that seeing title triumph dissolve into title heartbreak in the flicker of an eye was a desperate blow for all of us. The dressing-room mood afterwards was one of sheer disbelief. We had wanted so badly to stand the championship trophy beside the FA Cup but it wasn't to be.

2: Liverpool 3 Crystal Palace 4 – April 1990

In boxing parlance this FA Cup semi-final should have been stopped at half-time. We had so much of the ball, so much of the play, it was embarrassing. It was one of the easiest first 45s I have been involved in and we really should have been six or seven goals ahead. But we went in leading only by a single goal and that was the problem. Our failings in front of goal allowed Palace to retain hope for the second half.

Within 40 seconds of the restart they were on level terms, cancelling out Ian Rush's opener. The game ebbed and flowed; we were 2–1 down, recovered to lead 3–2 and were then taken to extra time by a last-minute equaliser. Worse was to come in the extra 30 minutes as Alan Pardew scored from a scramble following a corner to give Palace an unexpected victory in a game they were struggling to stay in touch with early on.

This Villa Park game saw the two sides of me. It was one of my best-ever first 45 minutes on the ball but I was certainly less than satisfactory after that. In those circumstances you find yourself lulled into a false sense of security, you think nothing's going to go wrong and you become shoddy and complacent.

3: Arsenal 1 Liverpool 0 – May 1980

The marathon FA Cup semi-final: it took four games to separate us and was another heartbreaking way to go out, especially as we felt that, over the whole saga, we had enough chances to go through.

The way the administrators had scheduled the games was incredible. It wouldn't be allowed to happen now. After a 0–0

Robbie Fowler has come a long way since I first saw him at Melwood as a 14-year-old.

Keith Gillespie was the makeweight in the transfer deal which took Andy Cole to Manchester United, but the Newcastle winger has since become one of the trickiest in the game.

Chris Waddle, the outstanding winger since 1990, holds off Steve Staunton, the Aston Villa defender and Graeme Souness' most expensive mistake as Liverpool manager.

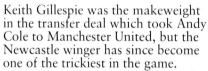

Gary Pallister rarely makes a mistake; the number one central defender of the early 90's.

Paul McGrath shadows Jurgen Klinsmann. The Republic of Ireland defender has been a stalwart through two decades.

Paul Scholes brings the ball under control but it is his movement off the ball which marks him out as an intelligent striker.

Jairzinho, the Brazilian winger, escapes from his Italian markers in the 1970 World Cup final.

Eric Cantona made a big difference to Manchester United and helped land their first championship trophy for 26 years.

Football was always fun for Pele, the greatest there has ever been.

Captain Courageous: Bryan Robson's enthusiasm and commitment brought him many injuries. A broken arm forced him out of the 1986 World Cup finals.

Sol Campbell – his strength, pace and versatility made him a first-team regular for Tottenham at a young age.

John Barnes – a magnificent winger who later became an outstanding midfield passer. He also scored memorable goals like this one against Tottenham.

Steve Nicol was a funny man and a fantastic full-back.

Gary Neville prepares for a long throw, just one of this defender's many attributes.

Carlos Alberto: one of the greatest full-backs of the last 25 years and captain of the brilliant 1970 Brazilians.

Peter Schmeichel: one of the world's finest goalkeepers and one of the best foreign signings.

Paolo Maldini showing the style that has made him an oustanding full-back and central defender for Italy.

Brian Laudrup deserves praise for the way he has adapted to the pace of the Scottish game.

Mr Consistency – Denis Irwin has been a model performer for Manchester United and the best full-back of the early 90's.

Jurgen Klinsmann with Ossie Ardiles in happier times for the former Spurs manager.

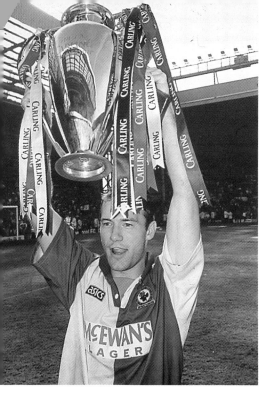

Alan Shearer with the Premiership trophy – few players have contributed so much to bring success to their team.

One more medal to add to Kenny Dalglish's collection, this one commemorating his 100th Scottish cap.

Bobby Moore and the World Cup-winning boys of '66.

opener at Hillsborough we went to Villa Park for the replay which was tied at 1–1 after extra time. Inevitably we were going for the championship as well and on the Saturday travelled to Crystal Palace for a 0–0 draw. On the Monday we were back at Villa Park for the second replay – again extra time could not separate us as we fought out another 1–1 stalemate.

The tie to decide who would meet West Ham at Wembley then went to Coventry on the Thursday where a Brian Talbot header, taking advantage, ironically, of a mistake by our former Arsenal player Ray Kennedy, killed us off. It was a desperately disappointing outcome because not only had we been the better side but, on a personal note, I was still waiting to play in an FA Cup Final.

We weren't allowed to dwell on our disappointment, enjoying a rest for all of one day before re-emerging at Anfield to try and wrap up the championship against Aston Villa. We won 4–1 which was just as well because otherwise we would have been faced with attempting to win it at Middlesbrough on the following Tuesday. Someone certainly believed in making us work for our money!

Clearly the effort took its toll on Arsenal who were beaten by Second Division West Ham at Wembley and looked thoroughly shattered.

4: Manchester United 1 Liverpool 0 – April 1979

This was my first FA Cup semi-final and it was hugely disappointing to be beaten. At the time you are not to know what other opportunities lie around the corner. I certainly didn't assume we would win through to Wembley as many times as we did in the eighties.

It's always worse to lose in the semi-final than at Wembley and this was especially galling because that year Liverpool were stronger than at any other time in my stay there. We were winning the championship by a country mile when we went to Maine Road for the semi-final. Six minutes from time I equalised to force a replay. It was a seesaw affair; we had gone in front, missed a penalty and then clawed our way back to finish 2–2.

In the second game at Goodison Park we again had a lot of the play but Manchester United did not lack for desire and spirit and Jimmy Greenhoff grabbed the only goal to knock us out.

5: Wimbledon 1 Liverpool 0 – May 1988

The championship was ours for another season, we had enjoyed a twenty-four-match unbeaten run, and in our penultimate league game thumped Sheffield Wednesday 6–1 at Hillsborough. We went to Wembley for the FA Cup Final, studied the Wimbledon line-up, and without being complacent, because the management would never allow us to take anything for granted, were left thinking we would have to be diabolically bad to lose.

And we were. Seven or eight of us just did not perform on the day and we got turned over, deservedly so, Lawrie Sanchez earning himself a place in football folklore by steering home Wimbledon's winner from Dennis Wise's free-kick.

We could point to excuses. There was the nonsensical refereeing decision which ruled out a Peter Beardsley goal when Brian Hill decided to bring play back for a free-kick – in our favour! We also missed a penalty. Normally you could bank on John Aldridge putting them away but Dave Beasant became the first goalkeeper to save from the spot at Wembley in an FA Cup Final.

Nevertheless, the fact of the matter is that you could be playing anywhere in the world against any opposition and if seven or eight players decide to go missing and don't play as they can then you will struggle, no matter the advantage you might have in individual ability.

A lot was made of the fact that Wimbledon had psyched us out of it by the shouting that went on in the tunnel before the start. Nothing that happened there contributed to the defeat but certainly their antics left a bad taste. In Rome before the 1984 European Cup Final we were noisy and exuberant but it was happy-go-lucky stuff. This was something else besides and I think the Wimbledon manager Bobby Gould should have taken steps to stop it. I'm not suggesting for one moment that it should be all nicey-nicey and gentlemanly and clearly it was part of the Wimbledon plan to pump themselves up. But on an occasion like an FA Cup Final such behaviour is not appropriate.

6: Flamengo 3 Liverpool 0 – December 1981

Our preparation for the world club championship in Tokyo was hardly first-class. We played on the Tuesday, travelled on the Wednesday, arrived Thursday and when we walked out for the game on Sunday our minds were still not properly tuned in.

Flamengo had been slightly better prepared – they had arrived two and a half weeks before! So we were always going to be up against it. Then Bob Paisley made one of his few mistakes as a manager, telling us not to get involved in a war. He was right on that score: we couldn't get near the Brazilians and hardly offered a tackle.

We came in at half-time 3–0 down and Paisley let rip: 'When I said don't get involved in a war I did not mean that you shouldn't go out there and compete,' he protested. Having said that, it was a game we could never have won because our preparation was so poor. It was a disappointment – in a contest to discover the world's best club side we weren't able to do ourselves justice. If we had had the same time as the Brazilians to recover from our previous game and prepare for this one, we would have had a chance of coming out on top.

TOMORROW'S WORLD BEATERS

The first piece of advice I would give any young player with ambitions to become a professional footballer is to make sure you are adept with both feet. It is a huge advantage. Sometimes I am embarrassed when I watch players who have just come into the England set-up who can't do a thing with their weaker foot.

You only have to look at David Ginola for proof that being able to play off both sides gives the man on the ball a head start over his opponent. With two good feet you don't need exceptional pace. Simply stepping from one foot to the other will create enough room for a telling cross.

Comparing eras is always dangerous. Those from the sixties will argue they were better than the seventies who will say it was better then than in the eighties and so it goes on. But I don't think the standard of today's domestic football can compare with the golden era for British clubs in Europe from 1976–84. Between Liverpool, Nottingham Forest and Aston Villa, we dominated the European Cup. Now our sides are getting knocked out early, and not even by those teams with a chance of winning the competition. They are losing to mediocrity.

There are laudable moves to improve the standard of young players but it won't happen overnight or even in the next couple of years. It is a long-term thing – you have to look to the next generation. It is vital to get hold of the players at an early age – there is no point in starting to coach, say, a 19-year-old because by then bad habits are ingrained.

Paul Scholes

Whenever I hear discussions comparing the merits of the British player with those from abroad, the debate always seems to come down to our inferior technique. For me the most obvious difference is the superior movement of the foreign player.

When I have seen Scholes play for Manchester United, his movement off the ball has been exceptional. He seems to have all the attributes you need to be a top-class player. He knows when and where to run – at 21 he has an experienced head and his finishing ability is good.

The striking positions are the hardest for a youngster to break into and at Old Trafford it's going to be more difficult than elsewhere because they can always finance another big transfer move, but this young man's development was one of the reasons Alex Ferguson decided he could afford to let Mark Hughes depart.

Sol Campbell

Whether Campbell plays at left-back or centre-back you don't see many front players getting the better of him. He appears to be very sound and unflustered and if you can be that solid at such a young age the chances are your career will go from strength to strength.

Campbell seems to have been around for Tottenham for some time and has already clocked up over a hundred appearances and in different positions too. He can play midfield but I think his future is at the back. He never seems hurried, there is always time for him on the ball, but when he needs to make up ground on his man he does so with tremendous pace and determination.

Robbie Fowler

Fowler was just starting out on his career when I was finishing mine. As a 14-year-old his talent shone through and he now has the world at his feet.

When Robbie was training with the schoolboys on the adjoining pitches at Melwood, someone would usually point him out. Even at that young age he had a reputation as an outstanding goalscorer. You may have worried about his physical strength, because at 14 he was so lean and slight, but certainly you never worried about his ability to find space in the box – a very specialised art – or about his ability to make maximum use of that space.

You could argue that he ought to do more away from the goal, but if you are looking for someone to stick the ball in the back of the net then you have to play him. For goalscoring, he is already up there with the best.

Kevin Gallen

Gallen is a similar type of player to Fowler in that he seems capable of scoring tons and tons of goals. He's probably a better player away from the penalty box than Robbie and can contribute more to the team's link-up play, but the Liverpool lad is the more prolific scorer.

Playing off the back of Les Ferdinand, Gallen had an exceptional time of it in his first season for QPR. In season 1995–6 he was in and out of the team and not so effective, but that happens when you are starting out on the road. Sometimes you have to go backwards to go forward.

Gary Neville

To win an international cap in your first season is a remarkable achievement and shows how highly Terry Venables rates Neville. He is solid in his defensive work, composed on the ball, and will be a vital component of the Manchester United side for years to come.

My only worry concerns his positional sense. When I watched the video of Everton's FA Cup Final win over United, at the moment Paul Rideout put away his header for the winning goal I was still looking for Gary. Call it the exuberance of youth if you like but he was badly caught out. United's own move broke down and Everton came away on the opposite side of the field to Gary's right-back position. They attacked swiftly but the ball rebounded from the bar, was pinged about the area and still I couldn't find young Neville. Maybe he was off injured, I don't know, but I would like to know where he was.

Keith Gillespie

Defenders fear nothing more than speed and Gillespie has an abundance of it. Kevin Keegan took him as part of Andy Cole's move to Manchester United, put him straight into the Newcastle side and has never looked back. What a steal at £1 million!

Again, it's very difficult not to see Keith getting better and better. Ruel Fox had a good year for Newcastle but this lad's form meant that Fox could not get in at the start of the season. That's the true test of how well Gillespie was performing because Fox has since shown for Tottenham what a tricky customer he is.

Pace is only one facet of Gillespie's game. He has clever feet in tight situations, a cool head on the ball and the wit to recognise when it's best to cross early and when he ought to hold the ball for players to make their move. He also contributes his fair share of goals which, of course, is a help to any side.

1 Robbie Fowler
2 Gary Neville
3 Sol Campbell
4 Paul Scholes
5 Kevin Gallen
6 Keith Gillespie

FABULOUS FULL-BACKS

An important requirement of modern-day full-back play is the ability to come forward out of defence and double as an auxiliary attacker – especially when teams use three central defenders across the middle and push the full-backs on. However, defending remains the top priority. It's better to be a great defender and a moderate attacker than vice versa.

A full-back has to weigh up the winger's weaker side quickly and play him accordingly. Forcing opponents down the line or, alternatively, inside onto their poorer foot, is an art in itself and needs to be coached. If you study the successful full-backs, they are always tight near the ball or tight to the body. The secret is to make sure your opponent has only one avenue in which to travel but at the same time to make sure you remain close enough to win the tackle.

I see too many full-backs taking up the wrong position when the ball is on the opposite side of the field. It's easier to defend now because with the pass-back rule everyone holds the 18-yard line, leaving less space between you and the goalkeeper but more margin for error. Even so, time after time, when the ball is on the opposite flank, I spot the full-back occupying a position behind the centre-back and deeper than him. It means a forward coming through the middle on the blind side of the central defender will be played onside. If the full-back is square-on the attacker will be offside.

It is not a position that has produced many outstanding players over the years. Mick Mills provided sterling service for many seasons for Ipswich and England and it might seem strange, given that Arsenal's success was built on a disciplined, durable defence, that neither Lee Dixon nor Nigel Winterburn wins inclusion. After some thought, Rob Jones and Tony Dorigo just edged them out.

British and Irish full-backs 1990–95

Steve Staunton

Selling Staunton was the most expensive mistake of Graeme Souness's reign as Liverpool manager. He let him go relatively cheaply and then spent heavily trying to replace him. Steve can play in six or seven positions, he is still only 27 and can be as good as he wants to be. His best years have been with Aston Villa and some of his best performances have been in the colours of the Republic of Ireland but I saw enough of him at Anfield to know that he already had all the qualities needed to go to the top.

Steve's best position is full-back even though he has shown he is a very capable midfield performer for Villa and I have also seen him play centre-back and even centre-forward. He has a great left foot, crosses a good ball, gets up and down the line well, and wins his fair share in the air.

Graeme Le Saux

I rate Le Saux as one of the best buys of the last five years. He had great potential when he started out with Chelsea and has since gone on to realise all his promise at Blackburn. To pay only around £1½ million for a regular England international these days is good business.

Le Saux is quick, very quick, and wreaks damage anywhere along the left flank. He hits accurate crosses and sometimes goes on to finish off the move himself. He strikes the ball with power and accuracy.

Stuart Pearce

Pearce is an opponent to keep clear of at all costs. When you played Nottingham Forest you would try to avoid encroaching on his territory! He was a frightening proposition for any winger to face, tough and tenacious. He's a 90-minute man and will still be going as hard and as determined when you are 3–0 down as he does at the start. A great player to have in your side.

We can be guilty of going overboard with wingers when they first come into the game, hailing them as the next bright thing after only two or three good performances. The acid test has to be when they come up against the guys in this category. Give a Le Saux or a Pearce the run-around and then it's safe to say with some certainty that a fruitful career lies ahead.

Denis Irwin

Irwin is Mr Consistent; I can't remember him ever having a hard time. He finds himself in all the correct positions for a full-back, has the advantage of being able to operate either on the right or the left and his lack of height never seems to be a problem.

Willing and dependable, Irwin is one of Alex Ferguson's best-ever buys for Manchester United. Relatively cheap among a number of expensive purchases, you can't imagine a United team without him.

Rob Jones

In the Liverpool system Jones has to get forward as much as possible but his main strengths are as a defender. He is fast and can recover well. I watched him play twice in quick succession against Newcastle. David Ginola, who until then had been giving defenders a torrid time, hardly got a kick. Jones was on to him early and tight, stood his ground without committing himself to the tackle and came out on top.

Tony Dorigo

I keep hearing that Dorigo is not so adept at defending, that he is great going forward but less capable in his own penalty area. Because of that I have paid special attention to his defending and I can't spot the supposed weaknesses. Tony looks fairly solid to me and it might be one of those cases where he is so good coming out of defence and moving forward that it is assumed he must be weaker with the other side of his game.

Dorigo has genuine pace and can transform a game with a dynamic surge from deep to carry the ball into enemy lines. His delivery is good as well. Crossing or passing, he does not often waste possession.

British and Irish full-backs 1970–89

Danny McGrain

McGrain was so talented he could have played the opposition on his own. I faced him a few times for Partick Thistle against Celtic and I watched him at close quarters with the Scottish squad. The impression was exactly the same – he was a formidable individual.

Danny was great at getting forward and as a defender was totally reliable. He could look after the right flank almost on his own, doubling as a full-back, midfielder and even a winger on occasions.

McGrain would run through a brick wall for you and he was indestructible. Nothing seemed to stop him though he was astute enough on the floor to avoid the toughest tackles.

Phil Neal

Ultra-consistent and dependable, Neal had a superb knowledge of the game and of how the flat-back-four unit should play. He used his brain to good effect when Liverpool's opponents believed they could take advantage of his lack of pace.

Phil was clever at channelling his man inside or down the line. He was decent in the air and would pop up with his share of goals. His record from the penalty spot was exemplary and what's more he could do it under the severest pressure. It was his penalty which made safe the 1977 European Cup victory against Borussia Moenchengladbach and his goal which gave us the lead seven years later back in Rome against Roma. He played in all five of Liverpool's European Cup finals and rarely put a foot wrong. He was capped fifty times for England.

Steve Nicol

Nicol could play in six or seven different positions and his versatility tended to detract from his outstanding performances at full-back.

I missed nine months through injury in 1989 and when I returned I played nine games on the right-hand side of Liverpool's defence, the first time I had switched from the left since my first games with the club in 1977. Steve was at right-back and he finished the season as the Football Writers' Footballer of the Year. In every one of those nine fixtures I came off thinking I could carry on until I was 55 if Steve stayed at right-back. Two good feet, strong in the air, quick and dynamic going forward, there was no area of the game in which he was found wanting.

Stuart Pearce

I mentioned in the 1990–95 category what a tough, fearsome opponent Pearce is. Yet at the same time you don't become a great player, playing all those games in the top flight at club level and also for England, without other attributes and Stuart has those in abundance. He has a wonderful left foot which is seen to good effect in his distribution and his shooting as well as in his power in the tackle.

Terry Cooper

Another with a great left foot and strong pushing on into forward positions, Cooper was a full-back with lots of tricks in his locker. He could glide past people down the line just like a winger, which is the position where he began his career.

The Leeds United side of the seventies was a passing side and every individual was required to do his bit in an attacking sense as well as being able to defend, work and get stuck in. Cooper had both sides to his game.

Kenny Sansom

One of those defenders you look at and try to remember if he has ever been outplayed by a winger. There weren't many occasions, if any. Sansom made an outstanding contribution to a number of league clubs over the years and played eighty-six times for England: his record of consistency was remarkable.

His surges down the left flank were a thrilling sight particularly early on in his career with Crystal Palace when he was part of the Terry Venables 'Team of the Eighties'. He had good close control and could weave in and out to make room for the cross.

Rest of the World full-backs 1970–95

Carlos Alberto

Alberto wasn't the best defender in the world but as an attacking full-back he was in a league of his own. I stand by what I said at the start: even if they are outstanding going forward, full-backs will lose marks heavily if they rate as only average defenders, but I make an exception for Alberto. The team he captained

to success in the 1970 World Cup was unconventional in that
players had to perform a variety of roles and fill a number of
different positions.

With Brazil possessing so many flair players it was inevitable
that gaps would become apparent, and with Italy, their opponents
in the final, not employing a wide left-sided player, Alberto was
able to show his prowess further forward. Three minutes from
the end he scored a magnificent fourth goal to underline a truly
dominant performance.

Paolo Maldini

Maldini is good enough to win a place in two categories: at
centre-half and also at full-back. He is that special. He has been
the best left-back in the world for some time and in the 1994
World Cup he looked the best central defender there has ever
been. I can't remember one occasion when he was less than 100
per cent assured and comfortable in the situation.

Maldini can do the lot. His positioning is always spot-on and
he seldom loses out in the air. He knows when to tackle and when
not to. In America he looked the complete player and he astounded
me by revealing just how good he could be in the central defending
position.

Manny Kaltz

West Germany have made a habit of producing full-backs of skill
and stature over the years and Kaltz is part of a very select group. In
the 1982 World Cup he was feared for his ability to create alarm in
the opposite penalty area. I remember the then England manager,
Ron Greenwood, answering criticism about the 0–0 stalemate with
Germany and claiming his side's ability to prevent Kaltz from firing
over his crosses was one of their achievements in the game.

From England's point of view it was a negative-positive and I
recall Greenwood taking stick for saying it, but at least it helped to
underline the worry other managers had about the damage Kaltz's

right-wing sorties and his deliveries from out wide could cause. His value on the overlap was inestimable.

Giacinto Facchetti

Long legs gave Facchetti valuable reach in the tackle and he stuck like a limpet to the man he had to mark. He had pace and that meant no one could outrun him and his vision and tactical intelligence made him the most dependable of full-backs.

Strong in the air, Facchetti scored many goals with headers from set plays. He was superb in the 1970 World Cup Final and was a lone rock in Italy's attempts to resist the attacking waves of Pele and the rest of Brazil's unstoppable team.

Andreas Brehme

Brehme was an excellent defender who was an exciting sight when he came out from the back with the ball. He was comfortable on his right even though it was the left-back position he dominated for so long. In the 1990 World Cup he brought a touch of class to a very efficient German side.

Just about every game found him at his best, scoring three vital goals, including one against England in the semi-final as well as the penalty-winner over Argentina.

Berti Vogts

Vogts was one of the best man-to-man markers there has been. Against Johan Cruyff, the best attacker in the 1974 World Cup tournament, he showed how proficient he was, following the Dutch skipper all over the pitch in the final and never allowing him a moment to settle. The German system demands that markers stick like glue to their opponents and he was particularly adept at it.

Vogts was never a brilliant passer of the ball but he didn't have to be. He won possession and passed it simply, allowing the more creative players to take over.

British and Irish full-backs 1990–95

1 Denis Irwin
2 Graeme Le Saux
3 Steve Staunton
4 Stuart Pearce
5 Rob Jones
6 Tony Dorigo

British and Irish full-backs 1970–89

1 Danny McGrain
2 Steve Nicol
3 Stuart Pearce
4 Phil Neal
5 Terry Cooper
6 Kenny Sansom

British and Irish full-backs 1970–95

1 Danny McGrain
2 Steve Nicol
3 Stuart Pearce

4 Phil Neal
5 Terry Cooper
6 Denis Irwin

Rest of the World full-backs 1970–95

1 Paolo Maldini
2 Carlos Alberto
3 Andreas Brehme
4 Berti Vogts
5 Manny Kaltz
6 Giacinto Facchetti

Super Six 1970–95

1 Paolo Maldini
2 Carlos Alberto
3 Danny McGrain
4 Andreas Brehme
5 Berti Vogts
6 Manny Kaltz

BEST OF THE BEST

There are so many memorable moments associated with winning trophies: the sweet sound of the final whistle, stepping up to receive your medal, sharing jubilation and relief in the dressing-room afterwards. Then there are the night's celebrations.

But the best feeling of all, by far, comes the following morning. Your head is spinning, you've been up late, you've drunk much more than you ought, but still the sensation is quite majestic. And it gets better and better each time.

I experienced the feeling on no less than seventeen occasions and the next time was always the best. Losing in finals helps to make the winning feeling all the more special. Having said that, at Liverpool we had some great times in defeat as well. After the 1988 FA Cup Final we held one of our best-ever parties. We were hugely disappointed both to lose to Wimbledon and in our own performance but we had won the championship again that year so we decided we had enough excuse to go to town.

I've been asked whether I would rather be playing now when the game is flushed with so much money it hardly knows what to do with it all. But how could you buy the times I experienced with Liverpool? If someone was to say: 'Here's £100 million for your memories,' forget it. You couldn't put a price on the good times, the team-spirit, the sharing of the success. It is beyond value and something that will always be part of me.

Outstanding achievements 1970–95

Wimbledon

The Cinderella club have had their critics for the way they have chosen to play the game, but you won't find me weighing in. A favourite Liverpool saying is that football is a game of strengths and weaknesses – playing to your strengths and exploiting the opposition's weaknesses. Wimbledon have done that and it's been the basis for their success.

Love or hate them, no one can denigrate their feat of maintaining a place at the highest level for so long and with so many factors working against them. They have had to share a ground for five years and have been forced to sell their better players.

By a clever manipulation of the transfer market they have kept themselves in touch with the elite and have developed the knack of producing young players to take the place of those whose value in the transfer market made it inevitable they would be moving on.

Of course, Wimbledon have an *esprit de corps* that is second to none. It's a facet of the game that should never be understated. People who sneer at team-spirit are those who haven't been at a club where it exists. If you share that special feeling of comradeship and camaraderie you know you're in front before you start.

It's easily forgotten that Wimbledon only entered the Football League in 1977. By 1986 they had won a place in the First Division and two years later came the FA Cup Final victory over Liverpool. It was a magnificent achievement against the odds but it has to take second place behind their ability to survive as a premier-status club for ten years.

Nottingham Forest

Having been promoted only the previous season after five years in the Second Division, no one expected Forest to be crowned champions in 1978. Yet they were and what's more they won it at a canter, by nine points. The way they sustained their results was a body blow to all their closest challengers. Liverpool were their main chasers and we would look at the fixture-list and identify games where they were liable to drop points. However, right the way through they returned home from tough-looking trips clutching maximum points.

We kept thinking they were bound to stumble somewhere along the line but their momentum never dropped. They had a splendid team, Peter Shilton and Kenny Burns enjoyed outstanding seasons individually, but Brian Clough also had them playing to a system designed to extract the maximum from their diverse talents.

Forest defended in numbers, always had men behind the ball, and aimed to hit you on the break. Playing that way you have a fair chance of going on a long unbeaten run and between November 1977 and December in the following year, they avoided defeat for forty-two games.

Republic of Ireland

I don't believe I was alone in following the Irish in the 1990 World Cup as if I was a Dubliner born and bred. You always want countries and players closest to you to do well, especially if your own country aren't involved, but on this occasion there was more to it.

The circus that followed the Irish around, the fanfares, the support, the sheer innocence of a tiny country competing at the World Cup finals for the first time proved irresistible. Neutrals were carried along by it and adopted the shamrock for themselves.

I enjoyed the spirit and commitment that Jack Charlton's team displayed so evocatively. Their will to win for themselves and each other was immense but I can't honestly say I enjoyed their style of football. It was direct and without flair but it suited the players at Jack's disposal and it would be foolish to argue that they should have gone about things differently.

What is beyond doubt, however, is that no one can win major competitions like a World Cup adopting such basic methods. The farther you go the more skilful the opposition are, eventually someone will outplay you. Still, reaching the quarter-finals was a magnificent achievement especially when you consider that not one of their players would have made it into the England team.

Blackburn Rovers

It's easy to underestimate Blackburn's achievement in winning the 1995 Premiership. To finish ahead of the field just three seasons after promotion from the Second Division ended years of obscurity, is an incredible achievement.

It should not be devalued because of the transfer market muscle Jack Walker provided for Kenny Dalglish. It takes a lot more than bundles of cash to create winning teams and Kenny's contribution was immense. As mentioned before, would Alan Shearer have signed for Blackburn if it wasn't for the fact that Dalglish was there? Would he really have chosen Rovers over Manchester United and Liverpool? If you went to a club in the middle of the First Division and gave a run-of-the-mill manager £50 million to spend, top players wouldn't give him a second glance.

For sure, it can't be done without money. But Walker's largesse and Kenny's know-how were a winning combination and the players responded magnificently. They had to face a lot of criticism for the manner in which they achieved their victories and, at the end when they had to dig out winning performances when their earlier fluency had gone, the pressure was really on them. They hung on and were worthy champions.

Arsenal

The Hillsborough tragedy cast a pall over the entire 1988–89 campaign. That was a shame for Arsenal because their success in taking the championship with virtually the last kick of the league programme, and what's more to do it at the home of their nearest challengers, was quite sensational.

It was heartbreaking for Liverpool to come so close but despite our crushing disappointment you had to feel deep admiration for the Gunners. To win by two goals at Anfield was a tall order in any season but to do it with the title at stake and the pressure at its most inhibiting was something else besides.

We were unbeaten in the league for eighteen games before the final showdown. Arsenal had moved to the top of the table on 26 December and never relinquished that position even though, losing to Derby and drawing with Wimbledon at Highbury immediately before the visit to Anfield, suggested they had let us in through the back door. They gathered their resources for one last challenge, took it on positively and the championship laurel was their reward.

Manchester United

It has never been easy to win the double, and in an era of greater scrutiny, enhanced pressures and heightened physical demands through the increased pace and intensity of games, it is more difficult still. When United achieved the honour in 1994 they were some way in front of everybody else, winning the title by eight points.

The season had moved into April before United found a second opponent good enough to beat them. Their only two defeats before then had both come at the hands of Chelsea who were forced to suffer at Wembley as United romped to a 4–0 victory to stand the FA Cup beside the championship trophy.

It would have been the treble, the first time all three domestic prizes had gone to the same club, had Aston Villa not saved a surprise for the Coca-Cola Cup Final, winning 3–1 in what was a significant tactical coup for United's former manager Ron Atkinson.

1 Wimbledon
2 Nottingham Forest
3 Blackburn Rovers
4 Manchester United
5 Arsenal
6 Republic of Ireland

My most memorable achievements with Liverpool

1: European Cup Final, Liverpool 1 Bruges 0, Wembley 1978

To win the European Cup is something you don't dare dream about, certainly I never did. It is a competition steeped in history and tradition, a trophy enshrined in the outstanding feats of the great names of the past – Real Madrid, Ajax and Bayern Munich.

I can still vividly remember watching Celtic beat Inter Milan in Portugal on black-and-white television. Ten years later, in 1977, I was round a mate's house with a six-pack following Liverpool's achievement in Rome against Borussia Moenchengladbach, seeing them lift the famous cup for the first time.

In 1978, a year after signing for Liverpool, I was involved in the biggest club game of all. It was strange because forty-five minutes before kick-off, any kick-off, I was usually a bundle of nerves but for some reason this time the butterflies had left me alone. Don't ask me why. Then, twenty minutes before we were due to get out on the pitch, someone uttered the words 'European Cup Final' and suddenly it hit me. For ten minutes I was a nervous wreck and it went through my mind that this was not the time nor the place to make a mistake.

Liverpool played well and, luckily for me, I played well too. Not that it was an exciting match. In fact, I was never involved in a decent European Cup Final, they have all been mediocre games. The philosophy seems to be that if you concede a goal you lose the game, so everyone keeps it tight. Certainly Bruges had not come to Wembley intent on contributing to a free-flowing spectacle. Now I think of it, I don't really know what they were playing for because they got everyone behind the ball and jealously guarded the 0–0 they started with.

Kenny Dalglish scored to put us ahead and we were going along quite comfortably when, with eight minutes left, I hit a dodgy back pass that was intercepted by Sorensen who took the ball round Ray Clemence and looked certain to equalise. Fortunately for me, Phil

Thompson had read the danger, raced back to clear the ball off the line and rescued me from shame.

Even at the final whistle I could scarcely believe I was joining all those great names of the past in receiving a European Cup Final winners' medal. I walked through Wembley Stadium at the end with my eyes fixed to it, convinced that my dream was about to be rudely interrupted and that I would be shaken back to reality.

People have asked me whether I would rather have played in some glamorous European location instead of Wembley. It could have been staged in the local park for all that mattered to me. Its importance was as the final of the European Cup.

2: FA Cup Final, Liverpool 3 Everton 1, 1986

The first all-Merseyside FA Cup Final, my first FA Cup Final, always brings back special memories for me, especially as I had not been playing particularly well. I had just been left out of the Scotland World Cup squad and things were a bit up and down.

The Cup Final is a one-off, a unique occasion when form can go out of the window and tension can play havoc with even the soundest temperaments. A Merseyside derby coinciding with the Wembley showpiece makes the nerve-ends tingle that bit more. The build-up for this game began some time in advance and just intensified with each day.

It all worked out well in the end but for so long it looked as if the day would belong to the blue half of Liverpool. Gary Lineker beat me to a long through pass and put Everton ahead. They really should have built on that advantage but we held on and thanks to a pair of goals from Ian Rush and one from Craig Johnston, were able to run out comfortable winners in the end.

3: European Cup Final, Liverpool I Roma I (Liverpool won on penalties), Rome 1984

This was an unusual campaign because we started off all the important ties with a home leg, and, after outplaying Odense of

Denmark in the first round, played at less than our best and looked destined to be heading out. In the second round we played Bilbao and drew 0–0 at Anfield. They were a decent side but we went to Spain and beat them 1–0. In the quarter-finals we faced Benfica, won by just a single goal at Anfield when again they looked capable of turning us over, and hammered them in the return 4–1.

In the semi-finals we were drawn against Dynamo Bucharest who I considered to be the best side in the competition. We beat them 1–0 in the first leg even though they had five clear-cut chances and were some way superior. Away from home? The pattern continued with a magnificent 2–1 victory.

So we travelled to the final having already demonstrated our spirit and resilience away from Anfield. We would have to do so again because the fates had contrived a meeting with the Italian club Roma, in their own Olympic Stadium. It was a fantastic advantage for the home side – certainly we would have been delighted to take on anybody at Anfield in the final.

On the day of the game we were woken from our afternoon nap around a quarter to five. Word quickly went around among the lads to tune into channel seven on the TV. Three hours before kick-off it showed the stadium already three-quarters full of supporters. That was intimidating in itself. Just how much did these people want to win the game?

Roma had a good side with the likes of Falcao Cerezo and Conti, so to overcome the odds was a very worthy achievement. The match ended 1–1 and so went to penalties, a possibility we hadn't taken seriously until our final training session at Melwood before leaving for the game.

We decided to end the session with a penalty competition; our chosen five and Bruce Grobbelaar against five from the youth team and their goalkeeper. They scored five out of five and our players missed the lot! It was unbelievable.

Joe Fagan was exasperated and was heard muttering that he hoped it didn't go to penalties in the real thing. He turned to Alan Kennedy who had just missed four on the trot, always blasting to the keeper's left and always missing the target. He did it again against the youths and Joe, with some impatience, said: 'Why don't you try placing it to the keeper's right, just try something different.'

In the penalty shoot-out Graziani had just missed Roma's

second after Grobbelaar had performed his wobbly-legs cabaret. We couldn't add up and were standing around the middle not knowing what it all meant before someone cottoned on that if we scored with our final kick we would win. I couldn't help adding: 'Yes, but Alan Kennedy's taking it.' We weren't the most optimistic of spectators but, just as Joe had demanded, Alan placed his shot to the keeper's right and the Cup was ours.

It was a momentous feeling, and not the only time Alan Kennedy was to emerge as a hero on the big occasion. In 1981 in Paris he scored the only goal to clinch the European Cup Final against Real Madrid.

4: 1979 League Championship

European Cups are the icing on the season's cake but the bread-and-butter diet is always the League Championship. At Anfield we used our own points system as the campaign went on to remind us of our priorities. The title was worth four, the European Cup three, the FA Cup two and the League Cup one.

This particular season we scored 85 goals while conceding only 16 and I can't see any side repeating that feat. To be part of a defence that only gives away 16 goals in 42 games is a source of great pride.

It wasn't as though we were a defence-minded team – proof of that is shown by the number of goals we scored at the other end. That year Clemence could have brought along his sun tan lotion and cigars and put his feet up. We went on a run of about ten games where he hardly saw the ball.

It was the best of all the great Liverpool sides I played in – Clemence, Neal, Thompson, Alan Kennedy, Case, MacDermott, Souness, Ray Kennedy, Dalglish and David Johnson – and only fourteen players were used throughout the entire campaign. When I'm asked how that team would fare in today's game my reply is simple: 'Give us the medals now.'

The midfield department was a superb unit, complementing each other so well. Three of the quartet could mix it with the toughest but they all possessed enough talent to come out on top in comparison with any other engine room. The great part about it was that they could all contribute goals. Souness and Case could blast them, MacDermott loved to chip them in from all areas and Ray Kennedy was brilliant in the air. For a big man he found a lot of space in the penalty area.

Every member of the side was comfortable on the ball. In five-a-sides I would be in with Souness and Dalglish. I never saw the ball. Then there'd be another team with McDermott, Thompson and Ray Kennedy who could pass and move and play keep-ball all day long.

5: 1990 League Championship

This was extra special for me because I had turned 35 and in the back of my mind was the realisation that this was probably my final season. The year before I had been out for nine months and it looked like I would not play again because of my bad knee but I came back and played as well as I had ever done. I was beaten by one vote for the Football Writers' Association Footballer of the Year award, finishing second to John Barnes who by his own admission had not played nearly as well as when he won it for the first time in 1988.

I started the season quite well but then we went to Southampton and got beat 4–1. It could have been 44–1. They hammered us that day and I was particularly poor. Of course the papers piled in, saying I was finished, that my knees and legs had gone and how I would never be the same player. I resolved there and then that I wouldn't ever be subject to those particular headlines again and it proved a considerable motivating force.

We won the championship at home to QPR and during the game I picked up another injury, to my bad knee where I had had lots of problems since 1985, rather than to my good knee, my left, where the damage had occurred the previous year. It was chronic wear and tear. I came back in pre-season and had another operation but the problems persisted. It would be all right during a game but afterwards would swell up and put me out for three weeks.

I had a scan and although the surgeon said he had seen worse knees it seemed the problem would not go away. The long term implications were not good so I decided to call it a day. Looking back it was the ideal way to go out – my last game was a championship-winning occasion and ensured I had equalled Phil Neal's record of an eighth title.

6: 1988 League Championship

This was the season we went on a twenty-nine-game unbeaten run, equalling the Leeds United record. Some of our performances were magical – the 5–0 victory over Nottingham Forest in April was the jewel in the crown – and when Peter Beardsley and John Barnes were doing their stuff it was a joy to stand back and watch.

We were going away from home and scoring 3s, 4s and 5s. Did it ever get boring? You must be joking – you never tire of winning and the management are always working hard to clamp down on any sign of complacency. Every game the message was the same: the first fifteen minutes will be tense and tight so it's important we compete as fiercely as the other side. Eventually our superior quality should take over as they begin to tire.

SO NEAR, SO FAR

You don't always receive your just deserts in this game. Sometimes teams can be in a class of their own and still for one reason or another end the season empty-handed or with one of the lesser trophies. In all walks of life we always highlight the winners. Seldom are the also-rans given the recognition their efforts merit. The teams below, in no particular order, are those that for a variety of reasons could consider themselves unfortunate not to have achieved more.

Everton 1985

League champions in 1985, Everton were denied the chance to compete for the European Cup when English clubs were banned from Europe's club competitions the following season because of the Heysel Stadium disaster. It would have been great for Merseyside to have had two representatives in the continent's premier competition; in other circumstances I am convinced Liverpool would have defeated Juventus in the Brussels final and gone forward to defend the crown.

Everton had probably their best side for some time and, through tragic circumstances, were unable to judge themselves in the highest company. Certainly we would not have wanted to be drawn against them.

Their combination up front, Andy Gray and Graeme Sharp, were a match for anyone and behind them Howard Kendall had put together a midfield superbly balanced and skilful. Trevor Steven, Peter Reid and Paul Bracewell were all handy on the ball and could put their foot in as well.

On the left they were complemented by Kevin Sheedy, a luxury player in many respects but one who was so good on the ball, so deadly from free-kicks, he was often a match winner. To give away a free-kick anywhere near the penalty area was, with Sheedy's ability on the ball and Sharp and Gray's prowess in the air, just asking for trouble.

Ipswich 1982

The Christmas programme in the 1981–82 season found Ipswich several points clear of Liverpool and on course to taste championship triumph for only the second time in their history. It was the first season since the introduction of three points for a win and in the New Year Liverpool staged a fantastic run to take the title from them by a margin of four points.

Ipswich were a talented side – the previous year they had won the UEFA Cup – and they will always wonder how they let the title slip. They had two international full-backs in Mick Mills and George Burley, while between them Terry Butcher was rock-like in his defiance and Russell Osman was a sound defender who could also play.

In midfield John Wark scored goals for fun, Paul Mariner and Alan Brazil were a mobile, willing and intelligent combination up front, while just behind them roamed Eric Gates, one of the first in the modern era to find success in that slightly withdrawn role.

There were so many individuals to commend and that's always the sign of a good side. You can have a good manager, good support, a harmonious board, but when you cross the white line it is down to the players.

Tottenham 1986–87

David Pleat's first and only full season at White Hart Lane provided a wealth of entertainment for the Tottenham fans as they went close in all three domestic competitions. They finished third in the League, reached Wembley in the final of the FA Cup only to lose in a five-goal thriller against Coventry and were denied a Milk Cup Final appearance when Arsenal won through after a semi-final replay.

Spurs would have to ask themselves why they finished empty-handed that season. They were certainly good enough to win something with the likes of Glenn Hoddle, Chris Waddle and Ossie Ardiles offering creativity and attacking ideas. Then there was Clive Allen and his incredible 49-goal haul and, further back, Richard Gough and Gary Mabbutt, a steadfast defensive partnership.

By this time Tottenham had smashed their Anfield hoodoo. Until 1985 they had not won there since 1912, but there was still a big difference between a Spurs team playing at home and the one that travelled away. The truly successful sides can't afford to be that inconsistent.

It could be a London mentality because I remember West Ham suffering from the same thing. Liverpool played them at home in the mid-eighties and took the lead after about 30 seconds. At that point the West Ham centre-forward turned to me and said: 'Here we go again.' It seemed as if he was ready to throw in the towel that early in the game, hardly the kind of attitude that wins games.

Holland 1974

The Dutch won through to the World Cup Final in two successive tournaments in the 1970s and were unfortunate in each case to find themselves in opposition to the home nation. It doesn't need stating that that's a clear disadvantage.

It's a safe bet to say that, in 1974 in West Germany, had they played anyone else in the final, the Jules Rimet Trophy would have been theirs. They worked with marvellous innovation and improvisation and provided many of the tournament's best moments.

The heartbeat of the Dutch side was the Johan Cruyff–Johan Neeskens axis which supplied many outstanding goals on the way to the final. Cruyff had elusive, formidable skills while Neeskens arrived late in penalty areas to finish off the moves that his more illustrious partner had started.

Their play was built on the total football concept adopted by the Ajax team who had won the European Cup three times in a row. Cruyff and Neeskens couldn't, of course, operate alone and there was marvellous support from the dashing Ruud Krol, the wily midfielder Wim Van Hanagem and lively forwards Johnny Rep and Rob Rensenbrink.

Maybe, in the final reckoning, the first-minute penalty awarded by the English referee Jack Taylor did Holland no favours. It relaxed them so much that they started to indulge in their pretty passing patterns without attempting to go for the jugular. Germany replied with a penalty of their own and despite continuing to dominate after that, Holland were eventually beaten by Gerd Muller's goal.

Brazil 1982

These Brazilians played with the attitude that if they conceded three it wouldn't be a disaster because they were confident they could always score four. A wonderfully bright and inventive side, they were strong favourites to win the 1982 World Cup in Spain after surviving a brutal assault from Argentina in the second phase. It left them needing only to draw with Italy to reach the semi-finals.

However, their confidence was shattered. Italy tested the Brazilian maxim and ended up on top after an electrifying five-goal thriller, Paolo Rossi playing the hero's role with a dramatic hat-trick. It meant that the prodigiously talented Zico, Socrates and Falcao would not receive their rightful reward. As gifted as they were in midfield, the side was weak in attack and ultimately it proved to be their downfall.

France 1986

France can point to their 1984 European Championship victory but the big prize, the World Cup, eluded them either side of that success. They were unfortunate in 1982 when Patrick Battison's injury at the hands of Harald Schumacher tilted the semi-final West Germany's way and again four years later when they provided many of the Mexico tournament's finest memories.

France made light of the blistering heat and stamina-sapping altitude in Mexico City to dispose of Italy, the holders, in a display reminiscent of their peak two years previously, and then outlasted Brazil in a tie memorable for the quality of the football and the drama of the penalty-decider in which Socrates and Platini both missed from the spot.

Most neutrals hoped France would exact revenge over West Germany in the semi-final but Platini was held in chains by a dogged midfield and an error from goalkeeper Joel Bats put the Germans on the way to victory.

RICHES FROM ABROAD

It's harder for a foreign player to uproot his career and come to play in England or Scotland than it is anywhere else in Europe. The speed of the game explains why so many of our imports have struggled to come to terms with the move. It's so much easier to switch from quick to slow than it is from slow to quick.

But if our game has gathered even more pace in recent seasons, so too has the succession of players coming over from abroad. It has a lot to do with enhanced labour movement throughout Europe and the removal of restrictive practices but it is also an indicator of the lack of talent coming through in the home countries and the explosion in transfer values here.

I still believe managers would rather invest in the home-grown player because he will give you more than his continental counterpart in terms of commitment and willingness to play on with injuries. But if better value is to be had in the transfer market abroad, who can blame managers for casting their sights further afield?

A great example is David Ginola who has proved a snip of a purchase for Newcastle at £2 million. He has two deadly feet and can place the ball on a sixpence. The accuracy of his crosses was one reason why Les Ferdinand had such a prolific season. However, I would want to see the French star over here for more than one season before I could name him in this particular top six.

The same goes for Dennis Bergkamp and Ruud Gullit who have both made a huge impact in the Premier League. I wondered though at the start of last season whether tailoring Gullit's skills to a sweeper's role was best for both him and Chelsea and I thought he proved more effective when he later moved forward into a midfield role.

My worry is that Gullit's fellow defenders will believe they too can pass the ball as immaculately as he can and land themselves in trouble. One of the best maxims is: if you can't play, don't try to pass. The Premiership is a graveyard for sides who try to pass but haven't sufficient skill to carry it out successfully.

Players from abroad 1990–95

Eric Cantona

Cantona was the perfect foil for Paul Ince at Manchester United, inventive, creative and very strong. With all his extravagant flicks and killer passes it is easy to forget how strong he is at the back post. He is deadly in the air, finds a lot of his goals that way and gives United another dimension to their play.

Cantona has many qualities but when I first saw him play for Leeds I wasn't sure about him. My initial verdict was that he was going to be like all those other players from abroad – if things weren't going well, up would go the hands in frustration. The game also seemed a bit quick for him but he adjusted better than I thought he would.

For £1 million, the signing represented a considerable coup for Alex Ferguson. I'm sure he would have walked all the way from Old Trafford to Elland Road to clinch the deal when Howard Wilkinson said he was willing to trade the wayward French star.

I wonder what has gone through Wilkinson's mind in the intervening years. Cantona has prospered at Old Trafford as a front player or, more often, in that slightly withdrawn role linking the play between midfield and attack. It can only have added to the Leeds manager's frustration as he was forced to wait a long while before finding someone to take Cantona's place. However, that's a comment made with the benefit of hindsight. At the time Wilkinson insisted, and no doubt still insists, it was right that Cantona and the club should part company. Whatever the rights and wrongs, I know which club had the best end of the deal.

Brian Laudrup

Laudrup, who I included in the wingers chapter, has always been a player to catch the eye. I have long thought him to be a class act and the way he has performed for Rangers confirms that. The English game is quick but in Scotland it is quicker still and it is to the Danish international's great credit that he has flourished there.

Jurgen Klinsmann

Klinsmann's impact on the English game for Tottenham was incredible. Again, I go back to the fact that continental players have an understanding of movement, when to move and where to move, that is far superior to the British player.

Apart from his great finishing ability, defenders never knew how to mark this particular striker. If you ball-watched he would take you to the cleaners. I remember his first goal in this country on the opening day of the 1994–95 season when he gained a vital half-yard on Sheffield Wednesday's Des Walker, one of our best defenders.

They were both waiting for the cross to come over and Walker seemed to have the situation under control. Ever so subtly, Klinsmann took one step forward and three back. Hey presto! The cross came over and he had all the room he needed to plunder the header and win Spurs the game.

Henning Berg

Berg is one of the best defenders to have come from abroad and made an impact in the Premier League. A lot of them have found the game too quick and frenetic but Henning has pace to spare and very rarely loses out.

At right-back, as opposed to the central defensive position where Norway prefer to use him, he was one of the most consistent players in Blackburn's championship season. Fantastic in the air, determined, strong and more than useful on the ball, he has proved a splendid signing.

Peter Schmeichel

Schmeichel, who is included in the goalkeepers chapter, has everything required to be one of the best in the world – physique, courage and natural ability. He makes a formidable sight for strikers bearing down on goal, spreading himself with those big tree-trunk arms. Invariably the ball hits a part of his huge frame and bounces away to safety.

Bryan Roy

Roy began his career in Holland and Italy as a wide man but at Nottingham Forest he was converted to a central attacking role by the manager, Frank Clark, playing just off the main striker. It brought him considerable success in his first season at the City Ground.

He has clever, quick feet and can always offer his side something extra. His balance and movement are exceptional. Forest look to him for a little bit of magic to win a game and he often obliges.

Roy's partnership with Stan Collymore was of the highest order; they seemed to be able to read each other's minds and to work well as a combination, although as individuals they were also a major headache for defenders.

Sometimes I wonder if the depth of Bryan's commitment is all it should be. He might not be the easiest player for a manager to handle but that's what the man in charge is paid handsomely for and Roy wouldn't be the first to receive special treatment.

Players from abroad 1970–89

Ossie Ardiles

Ardiles obviously had good technical skills but those who played against him quickly discovered that he complemented them with an impressive engine. For a little fellow, Ossie was strong and could get up and down the pitch easily. As a combative midfielder, he would work all day. It was an important factor behind his success with Tottenham and one of the reasons he stayed so long in England while other foreign signings failed to last the course.

Ardiles was good on the ball, and could pass as well as anybody, skills that you take as read as far as the South Americans are concerned. He could also fill any of the midfield roles; at Spurs he was sometimes used just behind the front players, while later under David Pleat, I recall he occupied the deepest position on the midfield diamond, helping to protect his back four.

Ardiles had just won a World Cup medal back home in Argentina, the pinnacle of any player's career, when he arrived at White Hart Lane in 1978. The refreshing attitude he showed in his willingness to learn and adapt to the English game was to serve him well.

Frans Thijssen

About as English a foreign signing as you could wish for, Thijssen was a vital part of the Ipswich Town side who were a threat in all competitions in the late seventies and early eighties under Bobby Robson.

The Dutch international reminded me of an Englishman in his work rate and in the strength that he possessed. Wonderful ability on the ball, high-calibre passing skills and a willingness to compete, proved what a good acquisition he was for the midfield positions. He could play equally as well on the right or in the middle: a great player to have in your side.

Jan Molby

Of all the players I lined up with at Liverpool, Molby was probably the most talented. People say he was a failure and should have done more but to my mind that's rubbish. He played in our double-winning side of 1986 and certainly hit the heights, though I wouldn't argue that with his natural ability he could have made an even greater impact.

Another misconception was that Jan was too slow. In fact he was quick over the first few yards. What let him down was the weight factor which meant that while he could do the first three or four sprints well enough, by the time it came to sprint number ten he would be struggling to show the same degree of pace off the mark.

A superlative midfield distributor, Molby could caress the ball with the outside of his right or left foot. He was that good he should be talked of as one of Liverpool's greats but it won't happen because people believe he was capable of so much more.

Arnold Muhren

Along with Thijssen, Muhren gained admirers for his part in Ipswich's cosmopolitan midfield, but he was a complete contrast to his Dutch contemporary. He made his debut for them against Liverpool and Terry McDermott ran him into the ground. Muhren didn't know whether it was New York or the New Year and he came off the field looking a broken man.

To be fair, chasing and closing down was never his game and maybe he was trying too hard to make an impression on his first appearance. He certainly chose the wrong opponent for Terry Mac could run all day and night and then the next day as well. Muhren would get close to him, prepare to take a breather, and then find McDermott was off again.

On the plus side Muhren had a poetic left foot that was used to devastating effect for Ipswich and later Manchester United. I would call him a luxury player who was able to adapt and be successful in England, someone his marker had to get onto quickly. Given space, he could destroy you.

Ricky Villa

Another luxury player but one who had problems adapting to the English scene. Villa had massive talent but he did not have the same mental fortitude as Ardiles and consequently struggled to make the same impression.

But amidst some disappointment there were flashes of outstanding ability and the Argentinian was assured of a place in history with that wonderful goal for Tottenham in the 1981 FA Cup Final replay against Manchester City. He seemed to beat about nine players, retained his balance through a series of testing challenges, then coolly slipped the ball into the net. A tricky forward player with lots of skill.

Jesper Olsen

Olsen was an exciting winger who could make and score goals with a trusty left foot. He was swift over the ground, hard to button down, and had the ability to take players on and make space for himself.

The Danish international became a big favourite with the Old Trafford fans after Ron Atkinson signed him for Manchester United from Ajax operating either wide in attack or in midfield. One of his best performances came against Liverpool in United's FA Cup semi-final replay victory at Maine Road in 1985.

Players from abroad 1990–95

1 Eric Cantona
2 Jurgen Klinsmann
3 Peter Schmeichel
4 Brian Laudrup
5 Bryan Roy
6 Henning Berg

Players from abroad 1970–89

1 Ossie Ardiles
2 Frans Thijssen
3 Jan Molby
4 Arnold Muhren
5 Ricky Villa
6 Jesper Olsen

Players from abroad 1970–95

1 Eric Cantona
2 Jurgen Klinsmann
3 Ossie Ardiles
4 Frans Thijssen
5 Peter Schmeichel
6 Jan Molby

THE WAY TO THE TOP

Six assets needed to become a great player

Natural ability: First and foremost in importance because even with a surfeit of the other qualities listed, you are going nowhere without it.
Pride or hunger: There has to be a determination to give your best at all times and to make the most of your ability.
Dedication: A commitment to your career is important, particularly when you are setting out as a young player and distractions lie in wait. There has to be the dedication to work extra hard on your game when things are not going well.
Luck: Vital in every walk of life and professional football is no different.
Courage: Comes in different shapes and sizes. I was never the most courageous in terms of tackling but I played a lot of games when I should have rested my injured knees.
Listen and learn: Young players receive a lot of advice from older pros and management and it's only common sense to take heed. They have been in the game a long time and their experience can be beneficial.

Six assets needed to become a great manager

Good players: You can't win anything without them.
Knowledge of the game: Including being able to judge players' ability.

Strong help from the coaching staff: The way the game is nowadays, it's a two-man job at the very least.

Ability to judge a player's character: A dressing-room is made up of all colours, shapes and sizes and they won't all need the same kind of handling.

Ruthlessness: All the top managers I have known have not allowed sentimentality and their regard for players' efforts last season, last month or even last week to affect their judgement if they believe someone else could do a better job.

Ability to handle the media and the supporters: Management has become a very public occupation and it is important to have the media on your side.

CAPTAINS WITH CLOUT

There are two kinds of leader on a football field: those who shout and wave their fists in order to get more from their team and the quieter types who put their message across through example. I was in the latter category. You hear about buckets being kicked and cups of tea sent flying in the dressing-room as emotions come to the boil and points are made with vehemence, but I was never comfortable with that kind of approach.

It is designed to put the fear of God into the opposition but half the time it puts the fear of God into your own team-mates, and Liverpool captains and managers were always too wise for that. Never at any stage in my Anfield career did I witness anything like that before a game – on a few occasions afterwards when someone was not happy, but never before.

When Kenny Dalglish became manager and asked me to take over as captain, I didn't really want the job. I suppose it was a similar situation to the one he found himself in when Liverpool asked him to succeed Joe Fagan as manager: it was not an offer you could turn down.

Kenny's reason for choosing me as skipper was simple: he thought I was lucky. He considered I was lucky at everything. 'If anyone's going to get a break, Al, it's you,' he would say. I was sitting beside him as we were preparing for a pre-season game at Brighton when he said: 'You take the ball.' I thought, what does he mean, take the ball? Take the ball where during a game? Then the penny dropped.

I never considered myself captaincy material. I used to enjoy winding people up in the dressing-room and having a laugh and a joke; laying down the law was not something that came easy.

I was part of a standing joke at Anfield. When Graeme Souness was captain he seemed to have the knack of saying the right things. At that time, Joe Fagan and Ronnie Moran would be hard at work before games giving a pre-match muscle rub to those who needed it. Whatever Souness had to say would always produce a positive response from them. They would be falling over themselves to agree.

Yet if Ian Rush or Ronnie Whelan said the same thing they wouldn't get a reaction. Everyone would just ignore it and get on with their preparation. So I gave them the lines to deliver, inane, clichéd comments that didn't amount to anything, things like 'let's get after them'. If we were at Southampton or Norwich they would say, 'Let's not come off this pitch disappointed because it's a long way home.' Their delivery was absolutely hopeless and it would never have geed anyone up. Henry V and Agincourt it definitely wasn't, but it would produce a laugh and crack the tension.

When it came to my time to be captain I had a problem. I used to churn out the right words, try to look forceful and vehement, but deep down my heart was not in it. Deep down I was scared to death of the 90 minutes ahead.

British captains 1970–95

Tommy Smith was Bill Shankly's captain for a long, long time and there can be no more glowing tribute to your ability to lead the team. Shanks would not have allowed anyone to take on the role if they weren't absolutely dependable and didn't share the great man's unquenchable hunger and commitment.

Tommy was a hard man with a big heart. He wanted to play, hated being beaten and was an underrated player. He had a reputation for being tough in the tackle but that was by no means the only facet to his game. He was more than decent on the ball. **Graeme Souness** was from a similar mould to Smith, tough and demanding and someone who instantly commanded respect from his team. Graeme was a bad loser, a moaner in the dressing-room but only for the right reasons and when we were beaten. Before games he was good at those gee-'em-up one-liners.

A captain willing to keep going for the team through thick and thin, even if he's having a bad time of it personally, will find others responding to his example. It will have a positive, rallying effect on the whole team. **Bryan Robson** epitomised that for Manchester United. His Middlesbrough players will know the reputation he had as á 90-minute, never-give-up performer and that can only help him now as a manager. They know he will settle for nothing less than 100 per cent.

The prince of captains was **Bobby Moore** who had a regal presence on the field. He did not have to open his mouth to command respect, it would flow to him automatically. He was the kind of captain people would want to do their utmost for. He is still the only captain of a British team to have received the World Cup. I wonder who will be next?

Anybody who was captain for such a long time of a team like Leeds United, brimful of great players, has to be a forceful personality in his own right. **Billy Bremner** was a hero to millions of Scottish kids growing up in the sixties and seventies. League championships, FA Cup finals, European Cups, he was there for the lot, a big-time player who relished the heat of the battle.

Like Bremner, **Frank McLintock** was a fully paid-up member of the rolled-sleeves captaincy brigade, constantly demanding more effort from his players. He was part of Arsenal's double-winning team of 1971 and earned a reputation as one of the best footballing defenders.

       1 Bobby Moore
       2 Tommy Smith
       3 Graeme Souness
       4 Billy Bremner
       5 Bryan Robson
       6 Frank McLintock

A ONE-MAN SHOW

Six outstanding performances against Liverpool

We had gone fifteen games without defeat early in the 1983–84 season when we went to Coventry and caught a cold, **Terry Gibson** firing a hat-trick in a 4–0 win. It was almost unheard of for us to concede that many, and unusual for an opposing striker to enjoy himself to that extent. Gibson was quick off the mark and was one of those players who caused problems if he was allowed to get on the wrong side. Neither Mark Lawrenson nor myself could get near him that day.

When Tottenham won at Anfield in 1986–87 (the second time they had been successful there in three seasons), their tall Scottish defender, **Richard Gough**, proved to be a formidable opponent. He was imperious that day, winning everything in the air, and we couldn't find a way to get the ball away from him.

One of the reasons Liverpool bought **Mark Lawrenson** in 1981 was because of his terrific display when performing a marking job on Kenny Dalglish for Brighton in an FA Cup-tie at Anfield the previous year. We won 1–0 and I scored the second-half winner but our bench preferred to take note of Lawro's performance. He did remarkably well, particularly when you recall that the way Brighton played, defending the 18-yard line, they were taking away one of his strengths, his great recovery pace. It was his tackling, his closing down of Kenny and his strength that caught the eye.

Peter Shilton gave so many outstanding performances for

Nottingham Forest against Liverpool that it is not easy to select one. Even by his standards he was pretty exceptional in the 1978–79 League Cup semi-final first leg at the City Ground. We pummelled Forest but couldn't get the ball past him. He made five or six world-class saves that night and eventually had his reward when his side scored an 89th-minute penalty.

Glenn Hoddle was an artist who, if you allowed him space, would destroy you. He had masterful distributive skills and could locate colleagues with a 50-yard pass as easily as others pass it square over five. When we played Spurs in 1982 he had the best 45 minutes I can remember of any player facing Liverpool. The range of his passing that day was just incredible but fortunately we got to grips with him after half-time.

Both games against Leicester in the 1978–79 season were notable for the resistance of their goalkeeper **Ian Andrews**. He took it upon himself to defy everything that was thrown at him. I later found out that Liverpool had tried to sign him but after that his career did not seem to go forward in the way it was thought it would. His performances were as good as anything that the big names – Shilton and Jennings – produced against us and that says it all.

Six outstanding displays for Liverpool

Graeme Souness scored a scintillating hat-trick when Liverpool beat CSKA Sofia 5–1 at Anfield in the 1981 European Cup quarter-final. The Bulgarians were a half-decent side but they couldn't live with Souness's shooting power. He hit the first one from the edge of the box with some force; the other two he drilled expertly into the net from 25 yards.

To win through to the Rome European Cup Final we faced a difficult last hurdle against Dynamo Bucharest. They came to Anfield and although we beat them 1–0 they looked a tasty side and had about four great chances to score. So we were bracing ourselves for a tough encounter in Romania. **Ian Rush** scored a brilliant goal after 20 minutes. He went to hit it, but came inside the defender before chipping the keeper. He later scored a second which came as a mighty relief because Dynamo had equalised and were starting to put us under the cosh.

Kenny Dalglish produced so many excellent performances, how do you pick out the best? A difficult task but even by his standards his display against Arsenal in the 1979 Charity Shield at Wembley was exceptional. He scored the goal of the game, cutting in from 25 yards and shooting past Pat Jennings, and was the pick of a team display I rate as the best in my fourteen years at Anfield.

Ian Rush scored four against Everton at Goodison Park in November 1982, an outstanding achievement and the first Merseyside derby hat-trick since 1935 while our 5–0 win was the biggest away from home in a Merseyside derby since 1914. He also scored a memorable hat-trick at Aston Villa and five in a 6–0 drubbing of Luton but he never displayed sharper instincts than that day at Goodison.

Peter Beardsley chose the 5–0 thrashing of Nottingham Forest in 1988 to show what he was capable of. He scored one of the goals and made two others in a performance the legendary Tom Finney rated one of the finest exhibitions of entertaining football he had ever seen. Beardsley's dummies were exquisite – he was sending the crowd the wrong way as well.

Sammy Lee produced a vital marking job on Paul Breitner in the away leg of the 1981 European Cup semi-final which was all the sweeter for us because of the criticism the Bayern Munich midfielder had made of our performance at Anfield. Sammy never gave Breitner a kick and he was ideally suited to the role. It required a lot of heart and stamina as well as skill, and Sammy, an underrated player, was well served in all three departments.

EUROPEAN CHAMPIONSHIP HIGHLIGHTS

Best goal to win a final

The 1988 final brought together Holland and Russia, the surprise package of the competition who, in the group games, had humbled England 3–1 and included a marvellous trophy-deciding goal from **Marco Van Basten**.

The outstanding player of the tournament, Van Basten had missed most of the season through injury and began the competition in West Germany on the substitutes bench. When he was given his chance, he showed that his ability was unimpaired, hitting England with an outstanding hat-trick in the group games.

However, his best was saved to the very last. The final was in the second half, the Dutch leading by a Ruud Gullit header, when the ball was played in long and high from the left by Arnold Muhren. It was aimed towards Van Basten but appeared to have taken him too far away from the goal. The angle looked far too tight to contemplate an attempt on goal, yet the AC Milan striker recognised no such obstacles. The technique was faultless as he met the ball powerfully on the volley and managed to keep it on target, the ball arrowing in under the crossbar and into the far corner of the net.

Outstanding final

There have not been many outstanding finals and certainly **Denmark**'s win in **1992** over Germany could never be classed as the greatest of games. But the achievement of the Scandinavian outsiders made it a special event. Denmark's victory was well merited and well received, Germany winning themselves few friends in the final with the way they resorted to physical tactics.

The Germans had won a thrilling contest against Sweden in the semi-final, ousting the hosts by the best of five goals. Having lost their skipper, Lothar Matthaus, before the tournament began, they were further depleted when his successor, Rudi Voller, lasted just one half of the opening game before departing with a broken arm.

The Danes were also badly affected by absentees for the final. After John Jensen shot them ahead in the first half they were forced to absorb heavy pressure until Kim Vilfort scored with just 12 minutes to go and assured them of a famous victory.

Outstanding tournament

The 1984 tournament in France was well contested and featured a number of stirring games but the **1976** event in **Yugoslavia**, the first time a major international series was played in Eastern Europe, set a standard that has still to be matched.

It was a magnificent tournament with every one of the final games decided on penalties. You can argue all night and day about the method of deciding on a winner after two teams have tied, but you can't complain that it does not generate raw excitement.

Czechoslovakia began the qualifying series two years before with a 3–0 win over England in Don Revie's first game in charge and came to a peak with this tournament. After reaching the heights with a penalty victory after their final against West Germany ended 2–2, their team fell away and failed to qualify for the next two World Cup finals.

Greatest individual performance

Michel Platini was probably at his peak in the 1984 tournament in his home country. He scored goals and led from the front. He showed his team the way and they were keen to follow. His record was quite phenomenal, scoring in every single game.

France lacked a striker of international repute but more than made up for it with a superlative midfield in which Platini had smart assistance from Jean Tigana, Alain Giresse and Fernandez who could all hold their own in the highest company. But it was Platini who shone brightest of all, scoring the goal that beat Denmark in the opening match and firing hat-tricks against Belgium and Yugoslavia when France had trailed to the team who were to finish bottom of their group.

In the semi-final the reviving Portuguese took France to extra time before, inevitably, Platini won it. The neutrals had been hoping for a shoot-out between France and Denmark, the two outstanding sides, but the tiring Danes lost out on penalties to Spain. At least the final had a fitting conclusion, Platini maintaining his record by scoring in a 2–0 victory.

Outstanding winning achievement

Another vote for **Denmark** and **1992**. It was incredible to think that they hadn't qualified for the tournament and were only invited to take part twelve days before the start when Yugoslavia were ruled out because of the escalating civil war. So late was the decision taken that some of the Danish squad had to be called back from their holidays.

In truth, they began the event as though their minds were still on the beach. They survived an unimpressive performance against England and a defeat by the hosts, Sweden, before putting their game together against France with a 2–1 victory which ensured they went through at the expense of the two sides originally favoured to make it to the latter stages, England and France.

In the semi-finals the Danes really came of age when they fought off both crippling injuries and the talented Dutch. Ahead twice, they were eventually taken to extra time and then to penalties but weren't to be denied.

Greatest performance by a British side

The showing of the home nations in this tournament has been poor to say the least but the **Republic of Ireland** made it a memorable occasion for their supporters in Germany in **1988**, the first time they had progressed to the finals of a major competition.

It was a qualification against all the odds, for when their own programme had finished, their invitation depended on Scotland winning in Bulgaria, a tall order for Bulgaria hadn't been beaten at home and Scotland had no incentive to win beyond personal pride. Little-known Scot Gary Mackay became the toast of a thousand Dublin bars with his winning goal.

In Germany, Jack Charlton's side were drawn against England in the first game and won it with a looping Ray Houghton header. After that the Irish resistance held firm against incessant English pressure. The Irish went on to draw against the Russians, having led through Ronnie Whelan. The same result against the Dutch would have taken them further in the competition. They were holding the eventual winners, and relatively comfortably, until eight minutes from time when Kieft's viciously swerving header spun wildly off the turf and, unluckily for the Irish, into their net.

ALL CHANGE

Six changes that have been good for the game

Three points for a win

Increasing the value of a win has made the game more exciting because now teams can string a run of victories together and more easily make up lost ground in the table. Supporters can live in hope for much longer; theoretically their team remain in contention for honours much further down the road.

I'm not certain, however, that the switch has led to more entertaining football. I believe teams still go away from home with the determination not to get beaten uppermost in their minds rather than gambling on an extra man in attack to secure all three points.

The way I would sum it up is that psychologically the difference between drawing and winning is not that great whereas the difference between drawing and losing is huge. Training on a Monday morning is shrouded in doom and gloom if you lost on the Saturday. Win or draw and the atmosphere is so different.

Formation of the Premier League

The formation of the new elite league has been an overwhelming success, attracting new money into the game and securing a transformation in our grounds. The switch to all-seater stadiums has been long overdue – in a modern world it is the only way to watch a game.

Naturally in Liverpool there was opposition when it was decided to pull down the Kop, an institution revered by generations of Liverpudlians and a monument to a city's abiding love for its club. However, I'm convinced there would now be majority support for the redevelopment work.

Although the Premier League has attracted a lot of new money that was not the prime object of the exercise. I am against changes that are made purely with the object of raising money. Ask yourself what has been lost to the game because of the introduction of the Premier League. I can't think that anything has.

Reduction to a twenty-club top division

Any moves to reduce the workload on players have to be welcomed. To expect the best players to play forty-two league fixtures when they were also involved in cup runs and international games was unreasonable. Bringing the numbers down still further to eighteen would be another important step and help the home countries achieve more success in the international arena.

European Champions League

Changing the early rounds of the European Cup to a league format has, I think, produced more open games because teams put more emphasis now on trying to win the away games. Previously, it was custom and practice that, in a two-legged tie, the visiting side in the first game would attempt to keep things tight and hope to take advantage in the return back on familiar territory.

Now the philosophy is such that a draw away from home might not be good enough if other sides in the group are winning on their travels. It also gives more chance of the latter stages being contested by the best teams with less opportunity for the shock results that can always happen in the knock-out rounds.

Extra substitutes

The more substitutes the better as far as I am concerned and the switch to having five on the bench is a good idea. It means more players can be involved, which helps them; it benefits managers by keeping more players happy in a big squad, which is a must nowadays for those clubs with serious designs on winning trophies.

In addition, it means we no longer have that unhappy situation where players are forced to stay on the pitch with an injury because the substitutes have already been used.

Free Saturdays before internationals

There's no doubt in my mind that success in international competitions has a huge effect on the domestic game and for that reason we should be doing everything in our power to help our representative sides. Closing down the league programme in advance of an international is one such way.

It benefits the players because it means they are not turning out tired, it helps the managers because they have more time to work on tactics and it means supporters will see better performances from players who might, in any case, have been out injured had they been required to turn out for their clubs the previous weekend.

Six not-so-good changes

Outlawing the back-pass

Had this change been introduced earlier it would have killed off my game because I spent years passing the ball back to Bruce

Grobbelaar. My principal objection is that it doesn't make for good defending. Sometimes it gives the man at the back no alternative but to boot the ball into touch to avoid trouble when what we should be doing is promoting skilful defending and sound technique.

I wouldn't deny, however, that it has improved the spectacle for supporters because it keeps the game flowing. There's no doubt that watching the ball go back and forth to the keeper became pretty monotonous.

More yellow and red cards

I don't understand why players who have handled in the area should be sent off as well as concede a penalty. It's a double punishment and that's unfair. Anyone who has played the game will know that if you are the last man and the ball is about to go into the net and you are unable to stop it legally, the natural instinct is to stick out an arm and use your hands. On most occasions there is not time to think about the consequences and a possible red card.

The FIFA-inspired crackdown on bookable offences which followed the World Cup in America has been disastrous because so often genuine tackles end up with a yellow card. On the other hand, you see dangerous offences going unchecked; the balance is often wrong.

So much appears to be left now to the interpretation of the referee and that's where the problem lies because one man's interpretation will be different from the next man's. As soon as it's no longer a black-and-white situation then problems will occur.

Play-offs

To my mind Wembley should be left solely for the cup finals. Now it seems that anyone can play there and it has removed some of the old stadium's mystique. People might think that it's OK for me to say that having played at Wembley several times, but it took me nine years to appear there in an FA Cup Final and when I finally made it, the feeling was extra special.

I am not happy with the concept of the play-offs. It seems to be purely a money-making exercise and there is too much of that nowadays. It is wrong that you can finish in third place, say, 15 points ahead of your nearest challengers only to lose to them in a play-off. The clubs like it because it produces extra revenue and creates additional interest for supporters, but it is a change that is flawed if the most successful sides over the league programme don't receive their rightful rewards.

Number crazy

It is time we reverted to the old shirt numbers and restricted those performing out on the field to 1 to 11. The situation has got out of hand; I have seen players wearing a 26 or higher and it's become a nonsense.

Kit changes

There are far too many kit changes. The kids want to keep up with their favourite team and they demand the latest strip, forcing Mum and Dad to dip into their pockets again. A kit change every three years or so is acceptable but in some cases, it seems like there's a change every season.

Half-time interval

I've heard managers say they're unhappy with the extension of the half-time interval to fifteen minutes and I'd agree with them. It can change the course of a game because a team might be playing well, come in for what is now quite a long break, and find they are unable to pick up their rhythm again.

What you don't want is players and managers hanging around the dressing-room, whiling away the minutes until the buzzer goes. That's not the point of the exercise at all. Ten minutes used to be ideal. It gave you time for a cup of tea and for the manager to put things straight and then out you would go again.

GLOSSARY

ADAMS, Tony
Birthdate: 10.10.66
Club(s): Arsenal
Country: England
Caps: current player

ALBERTO, Torres Carlos
Birthdate: 17.07.44
Club(s): Fluminense, Santos
Country: Brazil
Caps: 72

ALDRIDGE, John
Birthdate: 18.09.58
Club(s): Newport County, Oxford
United, Liverpool, Real Sociedad (Sp),
Tranmere Rovers
Country: Rep Ireland
Caps: current player

ANDERTON, Darren
Birthdate: 03.03.72
Club(s): Portsmouth, Tottenham
Hotspur
Country: England
Caps: current player

ANDREWS, Ian
Birthdate: 01.12.64
Club(s): Leicester City, Swindon
Town, Celtic, Leeds United,
Southampton, Bournemouth
Country: England Under-21
Caps: current player

ARDILES, Osvaldo Cesar 'Ossie'
Birthdate: 03.08.52
Club(s): Huracan (Arg), Tottenham
Hotspur, Paris Saint-Germain (Fr),
Tottenham Hotspur, Queens Park
Rangers. Manager: Swindon Town,
Newcastle United, Tottenham
Hotspur, Guadalajara (Mex)
Country: Argentina
Caps: 51

ATKINSON, Dalian
Birthdate: 21.03.68
Club(s): Ipswich Town, Sheffield
Wednesday, Real Sociedad (Sp),
Aston Villa, Fenerbahce (Tur)
Country: England
Caps: current player

BAGGIO, Roberto
Birthdate: 18.02.67
Club(s): Lanerossi Vicenza,
Fiorentina, Juventus, Milan
Country: Italy
Caps: current player

BALL, Alan
Birthdate: 12.05.45
Club(s): Blackpool, Everton, Arsenal, Southampton, Blackpool, Vancouver (Can), Southampton, Bristol Rovers
Country: England
Caps: 72

BANKS, Gordon
Birthdate: 30.12.37
Club(s): Chesterfield, Leicester City, Stoke City, Fort Lauderdale Strikers (US)
Country: England
Caps: 73

BARNES, John
Birthdate: 07.11.63
Club(s): Watford, Liverpool
Country: England
Caps: current player

BARESI, Franco
Birthdate: 08.05.60
Club(s): Milan
Country: Italy
Caps: 81

BEARDSLEY, Peter
Birthdate: 18.01.61
Club(s): Carlisle United, Vancouver Whitecaps (Can), Manchester United, Newcastle United, Liverpool, Everton, Newcastle United
Country: England
Caps: current player

BEATTIE, Kevin
Birthdate: 18.12.53
Club(s): Ipswich Town, Colchester United, Middlesbrough
Country: England
Caps: 9

BECKENBAUER, Franz
Birthdate: 11.09.45
Club(s): Bayern Munich, New York Cosmos (US), Hamburg. Manager: Germany, Marseille (Fr), Bayern Munich.
Country: Germany
Caps: 103

BERG, Henning
Birthdate: 01.09.69
Club(s): Lillestrom, Blackburn Rovers
Country: Norway
Caps: current player

BEST, George
Birthdate: 22.05.46
Club(s): Manchester United, Fulham, Los Angeles Aztecs (US), Fort Lauderdale Strikers (US), Hibernian, San Jose Earthquakes (US), Bournemouth
Country: Northern Ireland
Caps: 37

BONDS, Billy
Birthdate: 17.09.46
Club(s): Charlton Athletic, West Ham United. Manager: West Ham United
Country: England
Caps: Under-23

BOSSIS, Maxime
Birthdate: 26.06.55
Club(s): Nantes, Racing Paris
Country: France
Caps: 76

BRADY, Liam
Birthdate: 13.02.56
Club(s): Arsenal, Juventus (It), Sampdoria (It), Internazionale (It), Ascoli (It), West Ham United
Country: Rep Ireland
Caps: 72

BREHME, Andreas
Birthdate: 09.11.60
Club(s): Saarbrucken, Kaiserslautern,

Bayern Munich, Internazionale (It),
Zaragoza (Sp), Kaiserlautern
Country: Germany
Caps: 86

BREITNER, Paul
Birthdate: 05.09.51
Club(s): Bayern Munich, Real
Madrid (Sp), Eintracht Braunschweig,
Bayern Munich
Country: Germany
Caps: 48

BREMNER, Billy
Birthdate: 09.12.42
Club(s): Leeds United. Manager:
Leeds United, Doncaster
Country: Scotland
Caps: 54

BROOKING, Trevor
Birthdate: 02.10.48
Club(s): West Ham United
Country: England
Caps: 47

BRUCE, Steve
Birthdate: 31.12.60
Club(s): Gillingham, Norwich City,
Manchester United
Country: England Youth
Caps: current player

CAMPBELL, Sol
Birthdate: 18.09.74
Club(s): Tottenham Hotspur
Country: England Youth
Caps: current player

CANTONA, Eric
Birthdate: 24.05.66
Club(s): Auxerre, Martigues, Auxerre,
Marseille, Bordeaux, Montpellier,
Marseille, Nimes, Leeds United,
Manchester United

Country: France
Caps: current player

CHARLTON, Jack
Birthdate: 08.05.35
Club(s): Leeds United. Manager:
Middlesbrough, Sheffield Wednesday,
Newcastle United, Rep Ireland.
Country: England
Caps: 35

CLEMENCE, Ray
Birthdate: 05.08.48
Club(s): Scunthorpe United,
Liverpool, Tottenham Hotspur
Country: England
Caps: 61

CLOUGH, Brian
Birthdate: 21.03.35
Club(s): Middlesbrough. Manager:
Hartlepool, Derby County, Leeds
United, Brighton & Hove Albion,
Nottingham Forest, England Youth
Country: England
Caps: 2

COLE, Andy
Birthdate: 15.10.71
Club(s): Arsenal, Fulham, Bristol
City, Newcastle United, Manchester
United
Country: England
Caps: current player

COOPER, Terry
Birthdate: 12.07.44
Club(s): Leeds United, Middlesbrough,
Bristol City, Bristol Rovers,
Doncaster Rovers. Manager: Exeter
City, Bristol City, Bristol Rovers.
Country: England
Caps: 22

CRUYFF, Johan
Birthdate: 25.04.47
Club(s): Ajax, Barcelona (Sp), Ajax,

Feyenoord, New York Cosmos (US),
Los Angeles Aztecs (US), Washington
Diplomats (US), Levante (Sp)
Country: Holland
Caps: 48

DALGLISH, Kenny
Birthdate: 04.03.51
Club(s): Celtic, Liverpool. Manager:
Liverpool, Blackburn Rovers.
Country: Scotland
Caps: 102

DASAYEV, Renat
Birthdate: 13.07.57
Club(s): Volga Astrakhan, Moscow
Spartak, Valencia (Sp)
Country: Soviet Union
Caps: 94

DORIGO, Tony
Birthdate: 31.12.65
Club(s): Aston Villa, Chelsea,
Leeds United
Country: England
Caps: current player

EDER, Aleixo Assis dos Santos
Birthdate: 25.05.57
Club(s): Atletico Mineiro
Country: Brazil
Caps: 51

FACCHETTI, Giacinto
Birthdate: 18.07.42
Club(s): Internazionale
Country: Italy
Caps: 94

FERGUSON, Alex
Birthdate: 31.12.41
Club(s): Queen's Park, Dunfermline,
Rangers. Manager: East Stirling,
St Mirren, Aberdeen, Scotland,
Manchester United.
Country: Scotland
Caps: –

FLOWERS, Tim
Birthdate: 03.02.67
Club(s): Wolverhampton Wanderers,
Southampton, Blackburn Rovers
Country: England
Caps: current player

FOWLER, Robbie
Birthdate: 09.04.75
Club(s): Liverpool
Country: England B
Caps: current player

FUTRE, Paulo
Birthdate: 28.02.66
Club(s): Sporting Clube, FC Porto,
Atletico Madrid (Sp), Marseille (Fr),
Reggiana (It), Milan (It)
Country: Portugal
Caps: current player

GALLEN, Kevin
Birthdate: 21.09.75
Club(s): Queens Park Rangers
Country: England Youth
Caps: current player

GASCOIGNE, Paul
Birthdate: 27.05.67
Club(s): Newcastle United,
Tottenham Hotspur, Lazio (It),
Rangers
Country: England
Caps: current player

GERSON, de Oliveira Nunes
Birthdate: 11.01.41
Club(s): Sao Paulo
Country: Brazil
Caps: 78

GIBSON, Terry
Birthdate: 23.12.62
Club(s): Tottenham Hotspur,
Coventry City, Manchester United,
Wimbledon, Swindon Town,
Peterborough United, Barnet

Country: England Youth
Caps: current player

GIGGS, Ryan
Birthdate: 29.11.73
Club(s): Manchester United
Country: Wales
Caps: current player

GILLESPIE, Keith
Birthdate: 18.02.75
Club(s): Wigan Athletic, Manchester
United, Newcastle United
Country: Northern Ireland
Caps: current player

GORAM, Andy
Birthdate: 13.04.64
Club(s): Oldham Athletic, Hibernian,
Rangers
Country: Scotland
Caps: current player

GOUGH, Richard
Birthdate: 05.04.62
Club(s): Dundee United, Tottenham
Hotspur, Rangers
Country: Scotland
Caps: current player

GRAHAM, George
Birthdate: 30.11.44
Club(s): Aston Villa, Chelsea, Arsenal,
Manchester United, Portsmouth,
Crystal Palace. Manager: Millwall,
Arsenal
Country: Scotland
Caps: 12

GRAY, Andy
Birthdate: 30.11.55
Club(s): Dundee United, Aston Villa,
Wolverhampton Wanderers, Everton,
Aston Villa, Notts County, West
Bromwich Albion
Country: Scotland
Caps: 20

GRAY, Eddie
Birthdate: 17.01.48
Club(s): Leeds United
Country: Scotland
Caps: 12

GROBBELAAR, Bruce
Birthdate: 06.10.57
Club(s): Crewe Alexandra, Vancouver
Whitecaps (Can), Liverpool, Stoke
City, Southampton
Country: Zimbabwe
Caps: current player

HEIGHWAY, Steve
Birthdate: 25.11.47
Club(s): Liverpool
Country: Rep Ireland
Caps: 33

HENDRY, Colin
Birthdate: 07.12.65
Club(s): Dundee, Blackburn Rovers,
Manchester City, Blackburn Rovers
Country: Scotland
Caps: current player

HIGUITA, Rene
Birthdate: 28.08.66
Club(s): Atletico Nacional Medellin,
Valladoid (Sp), Atletico Nacional
Country: Colombia
Caps: current player

HODDLE, Glenn
Birthdate: 27.10.57
Club(s): Tottenham Hotspur,
Monaco (Fr). Manager: Swindon
Town, Chelsea
Country: England
Caps: 53

HUGHES, Mark
Birthdate: 01.11.63
Club(s): Manchester United,
Barcelona (Sp), Bayern Munich (Ger),
Manchester United, Chelsea

Country: Wales
Caps: current player

INCE, Paul
Birthdate: 21.10.67
Club(s): West Ham United,
Manchester United, Internazionale (It)
Country: England
Caps: current player

IRVINE, Alan
Birthdate: 29.11.62
Club(s): Falkirk, Liverpool,
Shrewsbury Town, Dundee United
Country: Scotland
Caps: –

IRWIN, Denis
Birthdate: 31.10.65
Club(s): Leeds United, Oldham
Athletic, Manchester United
Country: Rep Ireland
Caps: current player

JAIRZINHO (Jair Ventura Filho)
Birthdate: 25.12.44
Club(s): Botafogo, Marseille (Fr),
Cruzeiro
Country: Brazil
Caps: 87

JENNINGS, Pat
Birthdate: 12.06.45
Club(s): Newry Town, Watford,
Tottenham Hotspur, Arsenal,
Tottenham Hotspur
Country: Northern Ireland
Caps: 119

JONES, Rob
Birthdate: 05.11.71
Club(s): Crewe Alexandra, Liverpool
Country: England
Caps: current player

JOHNSTONE, Jimmy
Birthdate: 30.09.44
Club(s): Celtic, Sheffield United

Country: Scotland
Caps: 23

KALTZ, Manfred 'Manny'
Birthdate: 06.01.53
Club(s): Hamburg
Country: Germany
Caps: 69

KEEGAN, Kevin
Birthdate: 14.02.51
Club(s): Scunthorpe United,
Liverpool, Hamburg (Ger),
Southampton, Newcastle United.
Manager: Newcastle United.
Country: England
Caps: 63

KEMPES, Mario Alberto
Birthdate: 15.07.52
Club(s): Instituto Cordoba, Rosario
Central, Valencia (Sp), River Plate,
Valencia (Sp), Innsbruck (Aus)
Country: Argentina
Caps: 43

KENNEDY, Stewart
Birthdate: 31.08.49
Club(s): Dunfermline Athletic,
Stenhousemuir, Rangers, Forfar
Athletic
Country: Scotland
Caps: 5

KLINSMANN, Jurgen
Birthdate: 30.07.64
Club(s): Stuttgart, Internazionale (It),
Monaco (Fr), Tottenham Hotspur,
Bayern Munich
Country: Germany
Caps: current player

KROL, Ruud
Birthdate: 24.03.49
Club(s): Rood Wit Amsterdam, Ajax,

Vancouver Whitecaps (Can), Napoli
(It), Cannes (Fr). Manager: Egypt
Country: Holland
Caps: 83

LAUDRUP, Brian
Birthdate: 22.02.69
Club(s): Brondby, Uerdingen (Ger),
Bayern Munich (Ger), Fiorentina (It),
Milan (It), Rangers
Country: Denmark
Caps: current player

LAWRENSON, Mark
Birthdate: 02.06.57
Club(s): Preston North End, Brighton
& Hove Albion, Liverpool
Country: Rep Ireland
Caps: 38

LEE, Sammy
Birthdate: 07.02.59
Club(s): Liverpool, Queens Park
Rangers, Southampton, Bolton
Wanderers
Country: England
Caps: 14

LE SAUX, Graeme
Birthdate: 17.10.68
Club(s): Chelsea, Blackburn Rovers
Country: England
Caps: current player

LE TISSIER, Matt
Birthdate: 14.10.68
Club(s): Southampton
Country: England
Caps: current player

LINEKER, Gary
Birthdate: 30.11.60
Club(s): Leicester City, Everton,
Barcelona (Sp), Tottenham Hotspur,
Nagoya Grampus 8 (Jpn)
Country: England
Caps: 80

LITTBARSKI, Pierre
Birthdate: 16.04.60
Club(s): Koln, Racing Paris (Fr),
Koln, JEF United (Jpn)
Country: Germany
Caps: 73

MAIER, Sepp
Birthdate: 28.02.44
Club(s): Bayern Munich
Country: Germany
Caps: 95

MALDINI, Paolo
Birthdate: 26.06.68
Club(s): Milan
Country: Italy
Caps: current player

MARADONA, Diego
Birthdate: 30.10.60
Club(s): Argentinos Juniors, Boca
Juniors, Barcelona (Sp) Napoli (It),
Sevilla (Sp), Newells Old Boys, Boca
Juniors. Coach: Racing Avellaneda.
Country: Argentina
Caps: 90

MATTHAUS, Lothar
Birthdate: 21.03.61
Club(s): Borussia Mg, Bayern
Munich, Internazionale (It),
Bayern Munich
Country: Germany
Caps: current player

McALLISTER, Gary
Birthdate: 25.12.64
Club(s): Motherwell, Leicester City,
Leeds United
Country: Scotland
Caps: current player

McDERMOTT, Terry
Birthdate: 08.12.51
Club(s): Bury, Newcastle United,
Liverpool, Newcastle United

Country: England
Caps: 25

McGRAIN, Danny
Birthdate: 01.05.50
Club(s): Celtic
Country: Scotland
Caps: 62

McGRATH, Paul
Birthdate: 04.12.69
Club(s): Manchester United,
Aston Villa
Country: Rep Ireland
Caps: current player

McFARLAND, Roy
Birthdate: 05.04.48
Club(s): Tranmere Rovers, Derby
County, Bradford, Derby County.
Manager: Derby County, Bolton
Wanderers
Country: England
Caps: 28

McLINTOCK, Frank
Birthdate: 28.12.39
Club(s): Leicester City, Arsenal,
Queens Park Rangers. Manager:
Leicester City
Country: Scotland
Caps: 9

McMAHON, Steve
Birthdate: 20.08.61
Club(s): Everton, Aston Villa,
Liverpool, Manchester City.
Manager: Swindon Town.
Country: England
Caps: 17

McMANAMAN, Steve
Birthdate: 11.02.72
Club(s): Liverpool
Country: England
Caps: current player

MOLBY, Jan
Birthdate: 04.07.63
Club(s): Ajax (Hol), Liverpool
Country: Denmark
Caps: 33

MOORE, Bobby
Birthdate: 12.04.41
Club(s): West Ham United, Fulham
Country: England
Caps: 108

MUHREN, Arnold
Birthdate: 02.06.51
Club(s): Ajax (Hol), Ipswich Town,
Manchester United
Country: Holland
Caps: 23

MULLER, Gerd
Birthdate: 03.11.45
Club(s): Bayern Munich, Fort
Lauderdale (US)
Country: Germany
Caps: 62

NEAL, Phil
Birthdate: 20.02.51
Club(s): Northampton Town,
Liverpool. Manager: Bolton
Wanderers, Coventry City
Country: England
Caps: 50

NEESKENS, Johan
Birthdate: 15.09.51
Club(s): Ajax, Barcelona (Sp),
Cosmos (US)
Country: Holland
Caps: 49

NEVILLE, Gary
Birthdate: 18.02.75
Club(s): Manchester United
Country: England
Caps: current player

NICOL, Steve
Birthdate: 11.12.61
Club(s): Ayr United, Liverpool
Country: Scotland
Caps: 27

OLSEN, Jesper
Birthdate: 20.03.61
Club(s): Ajax (Hol), Manchester United
Country: Denmark
Caps: 41

PAISLEY, Bob
Birthdate: 23.01.19
Club(s): Liverpool. Manager: Liverpool.
Country: England
Caps: –

PALLISTER, Gary
Birthdate: 30.06.65
Club(s): Middlesbrough, Manchester United
Country: England
Caps: current player

PASSARELLA, Daniel
Birthdate: 25.05.53
Club(s): River Plate, Fiorentina (It), Internazionale (It). Manager: River Plate, Argentina
Country: Argentina
Caps: 69

PEARCE, Stuart
Birthdate: 24.04.62
Club(s): Coventry City, Nottingham Forest
Country: England
Caps: current player

PELE (Edson Arantes de Nascimento)
Birthdate: 21.10.40
Club(s): Santos, New York Cosmos (US)
Country: Brazil
Caps: 92

PLATINI, Michel
Birthdate: 21.06.56
Club(s): Nancy, Saint-Etienne, Juventus (It)
Country: France
Caps: 59

REVIE, Don
Birthdate: 10.07.27
Club(s): Leicester City, Hull City, Manchester City, Sunderland, Leeds United. Manager: Leeds United, England, United Arab Emirates
Country: England
Caps: 6

RIVELINO, Roberto
Birthdate: 01.01.46
Club(s): Corinthians, Fluminense
Country: Brazil
Caps: 90

ROBERTSON, John
Birthdate: 20.01.53
Club(s): Nottingham Forest, Derby County, Nottingham Forest
Country: Scotland
Caps: 28

ROBSON, Bobby
Birthdate: 18.02.33
Club(s): Fulham, West Bromwich, Fulham. Manager: Fulham, Vancouver, Ipswich Town, England, PSV Eindhoven (Hol), Sporting Clube (Por), FC Porto (Por)
Country: England
Caps: 20

ROBSON, Bryan
Birthdate: 11.01.57
Club(s): West Bromwich Albion, Manchester, Middlesbrough.
Manager: Middlesbrough

Country: England
Caps: 90

ROSENTHAL, Ronny
Birthdate: 04.10.63
Club(s): Maccabi Haifa, Standard
Liege (Bel), Liverpool, Tottenham
Hotspur
Country: Israel
Caps: current player

ROUGH, Alan
Birthdate: 25.11.51
Club(s): Partick Thistle, Hibernian,
Celtic, Hamilton
Country: Scotland
Caps: 53

ROY, Bryan
Birthdate: 12.02.69
Club(s): Ajax, Foggia (It), Nottingham
Forest
Country: Holland
Caps: current player

RUSH, Ian
Birthdate: 20.10.61
Club(s): Chester, Liverpool
Country: Wales
Caps: current player

SANSOM, Kenny
Birthdate: 26.09.58
Club(s): Crystal Palace, Arsenal,
Newcastle United, Queens Park
Rangers, Coventry City, Everton,
Brentford, Watford
Country: England
Caps: 86

SCHMEICHEL, Peter
Birthdate: 18.11.63
Club(s): Hvidovre, Brondby,
Manchester United
Country: Denmark
Caps: current player

SCHOLES, Paul
Birthdate: 16.11.74
Club(s): Manchester United
Country: England Youth
Caps: current player

**SCHUMACHER, Harald Anton
'Toni'**
Birthdate: 06.03.54
Club(s): Koln, Fenerbahce (Tur),
Bayern Munich
Country: Germany
Caps: 76

SCIREA, Gaetano
Birthdate: 25.05.53
Club(s): Atalanta, Juventus
Country: Italy
Caps: 76

SEAMAN, David
Birthdate: 19.09.63
Club(s): Leeds United, Peterborough
United, Birmingham City, Queens
Park Rangers, Arsenal
Country: England
Caps: current player

SHANKLY, Bill
Birthdate: 02.09.13
Club(s): Carlisle, Preston North End.
Manager: Huddersfield, Liverpool
Country: Scotland
Caps: 5

SHARP, Graeme
Birthdate: 16.10.60
Club(s): Dumbarton, Everton,
Oldham Athletic. Manager:
Oldham Athletic
Country: Scotland
Caps: 12

SHEARER, Alan
Birthdate: 13.08.70
Club(s): Southampton, Blackburn
Rovers

Country: England
Caps: current player

SHILTON, Peter
Birthdate: 18.09.49
Club(s): Leicester City, Stoke City,
Nottingham Forest, Southampton,
Derby County, Plymouth Argyle,
Wimbledon, Bolton Wanderers,
West Ham United. Manager:
Plymouth Argyle
Country: England
Caps: 125

SMITH, Tommy
Birthdate: 05.04.45
Club(s): Liverpool, Swansea City
Country: England
Caps: 1

**SOCRATES (Brasileiro Sampaio de
Souva Vieira de Oliveira)**
Birthdate: 19.02.54
Club(s): Botafogo Ribeiro Prato,
Corinthians, Fiorentina (It),
Corinthians
Country: Brazil
Caps: 57

SOUNESS, Graeme
Birthdate: 06.05.53
Club(s): Tottenham Hotspur,
Middlesbrough, Liverpool, Sampdoria
(It), Rangers. Manager: Rangers,
Liverpool, Galatasaray (Tur)
Country: Scotland
Caps: 54

SOUTHALL, Neville
Birthdate: 16.09.58
Club(s): Bury, Port Vale, Everton
Country: Wales
Caps: current player

SPRAKE, Gary
Birthdate: 03.04.45
Club(s): Leeds United, Birmingham
City

Country: Wales
Caps: 37

STAUNTON, Steve
Birthdate: 19.01.69
Club(s): Liverpool, Bradford City,
Liverpool, Aston Villa
Country: Rep Ireland
Caps: current player

STEIN, Jock
Birthdate: 05.10.22
Club(s): Albion Rovers, Llanelli,
Celtic. Manager: Dunfermline
Athletic, Celtic, Leeds United,
Scotland
Country: Scotland
Caps: –

STRACHAN, Gordon
Birthdate: 09.02.57
Club(s): Dundee, Aberdeen,
Manchester United, Leeds United,
Coventry City
Country: Scotland
Caps: 50

TAFFAREL, Claudio Andre Mergen
Birthdate: 08.05.66
Club(s): Internacional Porto Alegre,
Parma (It), Reggiana (It)
Country: Brazil
Caps: current player

THIJSSEN, Frans
Birthdate: 23.01.52
Club(s): Twente Enschede, Ipswich
Town, Nottingham Forest,
Vancouver (Can)
Country: Holland
Caps: 14

THOMPSON, Phil
Birthdate: 21.01.54
Club(s): Liverpool, Sheffield United
Country: England
Caps: 42

TODD, Colin
Birthdate: 12.12.48
Club(s): Sunderland, Derby
County, Everton, Birmingham City,
Nottingham Forest, Oxford United,
Luton Town. Manager: Bolton
Wanderers
Country: England
Caps: 27

VAN BASTEN, Marco
Birthdate: 31.10.64
Club(s): Ajax, Milan (It)
Country: Holland
Caps: 58

VILLA, Ricardo 'Ricky'
Birthdate: 18.08.52
Club(s): Racing Avellaneda (Arg),
Tottenham Hotspur
Country: Argentina
Caps: 15

VOGTS, Hans-Hubert 'Berti'
Birthdate: 30.12.46
Club(s): Borussia Mg
Country: Germany
Caps: 96

WADDLE, Chris
Birthdate: 14.12.60
Club(s): Newcastle United,
Tottenham Hotspur, Marseille (Fr),
Sheffield Wednesday
Country: England
Caps: 62

WALKER, Des
Birthdate: 26.11.65
Club(s): Nottingham Forest,
Sampdoria (It), Sheffield Wednesday
Country: England
Caps: current player

WHELAN, Ronnie
Birthdate: 25.09.61
Club(s): Liverpool, Southend United.
Manager: Southend United

Country: Rep Ireland
Caps: 53

WISE, Dennis
Birthdate: 15.12.66
Club(s): Wimbledon, Chelsea
Country: England
Caps: current player

WOODS, Chris
Birthdate: 14.11.59
Club(s): Nottingham Forest, Queens
Park Rangers, Norwich City,
Rangers, Sheffield Wednesday
Country: England
Caps: 43

WRIGHT, Ian
Birthdate: 03.11.63
Club(s): Crystal Palace, Arsenal
Country: England
Caps: current player

ZOFF, Dino
Birthdate: 28.02.42
Club(s): Udinese, Mantova,
Napoli, Juventus. Manager-coach:
Juventus, Lazio
Country: Italy
Caps: 112